MONARCH
PRESS

D1111560

HOW TO SELL YOURSELF ON AN INTERVIEW

by Arthur R. Pell, Ph.D.

Monarch Press New York

Special thanks to my research associate, Hilary J. Pell.

Published by MONARCH PRESS
A Simon & Schuster Division of Gulf & Western Corporation
Simon & Schuster Building
1230 Avenue of the Americas
New York, New York 10020

MONARCH PRESS and colophon are trademarks of Simon & Schuster, registered in the U.S. Patent and Trademark Office.
Designed by Irving Perkins Associates
Manufactured in the United States of America
10 9 8 7 6 5 4 3
Library of Congress Catalog Card Number: 81-84565
ISBN: 0-671-43147-1

Contents

CHAPTER 1

YOUR INTERVIEW OBJECTIVE—TO LAND THE JOB

The letter of rejection staggered Paul. He had been certain he would get that job. His education, years, and quality of experience and his record of achievement in his most recent job made him a logical candidate for the position. What had gone wrong?

Each year thousands of well-qualified applicants fail to get the jobs they want because in some way they have not communicated their qualifications effectively in a job interview. Their resume and application form may tell a good story. Their references may check out extremely well. They may even do well in aptitude, psychological, or technical tests, but if they do not come across satisfactorily in the personal interview—which is the most important phase of the selection procedure— the longed-for job offer will not be forthcoming.

It is at the interview that the prospective employer determines not only if the applicant meets the job specifications but also whether the applicant has the personal characteristics that will fit into the image desired by the company. When there are several candi- dates for the opening, the interview enables the employer to compare each of them and select the one that best meets the company's needs.

To make the most effective impression at an interview, the applicant must prepare carefully. No interview should ever be taken without knowing as much as possible about what is wanted. And it is even more important to understand one's own background so thoroughly that each interview can be planned in such a way as to communicate this information in a positive and relevant manner for the job under consideration. It is essential that you know the objectives of the interviewer and fit your own objectives into that framework.

EMPLOYERS' OBJECTIVES

In most instances, the interviewer has either read your resume or the application form for the position, or both, and knows the basic outline of your experience and education. The interview will be used for amplification. In addition to the brief data most resumes and application forms provide, additional information regarding duties and responsibilities will be sought. The interviewer will want to know more about your education and how it relates to preparation for the job, as most application forms give very little space for this information. The employer will want to evaluate your advancement in both position and earnings.

Although most of the interview time will be devoted to discussing your job background, a secondary objective —evaluating your personal characteristics—will be built into every question and interpretation of your responses. Among the things the employer will be appraising are your attitudes toward your jobs, your employers, your direct superiors, and your subordinates. Interviewers will attempt to determine from the interview what motivates you, what your short- and long-term goals are, and what you have done to reach them to date. They are concerned with how you handle special problems on your job and what results you have had in resolving difficult situations.

Each job has special qualifications that may be explored at the interview. You may be asked questions to assess your creativity, your resourcefulness, or your ability to sell your ideas. Interviewers want to find out how you might fit into their organization in terms of your personality, ability to get along with others, and potential for growth. In addition, employers will try to determine your strengths and weaknesses and will try to get you to reveal negative as well as positive information about yourself.

Not only will they listen to what you say, but they will evaluate you on how you say it, what you do not say, and the nonverbal language you use. In brief, they want to learn as much as possible about your background, personal characteristics, and inner self in the short duration of the interview.

APPLICANTS' OBJECTIVES

Not only must you be alert to the employer's objectives when going on an interview, but you must also have a set of objectives yourself that should be kept in mind as you prepare for each of these experiences. Your most important objective, of course, is to *get the job.* To do this, your first subordinate objective is to make a good personal impression. Always remember the old adage that first impressions are the most important. So from the moment you enter the room, everything about you is being recorded in the mind of the interviewer, including your clothes, your smile, your demeanor, your voice, and what you say.

Your next subordinate objective is to present your background clearly, concisely, and completely. You must know your own background so thoroughly that you are prepared to answer any question about it without hesitation and in enough detail to satisfy the interviewer.

Another subordinate objective is to bring out your strengths in each phase of your experience or education and minimize your weaknesses. To do this you must be just as aware of your limitations as you are of your assets.

Most important of the subordinate objectives related to getting the job is to understand that there are probably several competitors for the position. Even though you do not know who they are (in most cases) and what they offer, you must be able to present your background so well that you will come across stronger and better than your competitors.

In addition to the key objective of "getting the job," there are two other related objectives you should keep in mind when being interviewed. One is to assure yourself that this is the right company for you—one that will meet your goals in both the short and the long run. The other is that this is the right job for you—one that will bring you up your career ladder.

With your goals clearly in mind and your knowledge of the company's objectives, you are now ready to plan your interviewing strategy. One should *never* go on a job interview without careful preparation. In the following chapters, we will discuss how you can assemble all the information needed on your own background. Once this file is prepared, it should be reviewed before *each* interview so that you are never caught by surprise with a question that you did not anticipate or for which you do not have a ready response.

It is also important that you learn as much as you can about each company to which you apply, so you can be ready to tailor your background to the needs of that company. This research will also help you determine what questions you may want to ask the interviewer about the company and the job.

If at all possible, rehearse for an interview by role-playing it with a friend or counselor. If your partner is an experienced business person, the role-playing will be more realistic and may help you by exposing you in simulated form to some of the tactics used by interviewers in the real job interview situation. Another good source for preparing for the interviews that really count is to accept opportunities to be interviewed by anybody who invites you for one—even if you are not interested in the job. These real-life encounters will sharpen your skills and make you more effective when faced with an interview for a job you really want.

CHAPTER 2

THE P.B.O.— YOUR PERSONAL BACKGROUND ORGANIZER

Whether you are preparing to be interviewed by only one company or plan to undertake an extensive campaign that may result in many interviews, it is essential that you be prepared to answer any questions about your background that may be asked. You should therefore develop a thorough summary of your qualifications as part of your resource material.

On pages 8–19 you will find a *Personal Background Organizer* on which you can list most of the information that is needed to help you prepare your resume, fill out company application forms, and most important, systematize the data that you are most often asked at an interview.

Think very carefully about each item on the P.B.O. before you write your answer. Little things about duties and responsibilities are often what make the difference between just doing a routine job and doing an exceptional one. If more space is needed to expand on any item in the questionnaire, use additional paper. It is better to be thorough than to miss the one point that makes you better than your competitors. Take all the time you need to do a complete job on the P.B.O. The process of thinking out the responses is in itself a valuable exercise. Writing down the answers in this systematic manner converts the exercise into a pragmatic tool.

Your Personal Background Organizer[1]

Education

High school: years completed ___4___

Special courses taken[2] BUSINESS MANAGEMENT

Special activities[2] _____

In what subjects did you do best? _____

What subjects did you like best? _____

What subjects did you like least? _____

How did you spend your summers when in high school? ___
WORKING, PLAYING SPORTS,

Part-time jobs when in high school _____
DISHWASHER, FAMOUS BARR

Special accomplishments during high school years[3]

_____

_____

_____

College, business, or special school:

Type of school _____

Name of school _SMSU_____ Degree _B.S_

Major or specialty _GENERAL BUSINESS_____

Special courses taken[2] _SALES, PSYCHOLOGY_____

_MARKETING,_____

_____

Special activities[2] _____

_____

In what subjects did you do best? _MARKETING +_

_MANAGEMENT_____

What subjects did you like best? _____

_____

What subjects did you like least? _____

_____

Part-time and summer jobs _____

_____

_____

_____

Special accomplishments during this period[3] _____

_____

_____

Graduate school (or post-college special schools):

Objectives of this training _____

_____

_____

School _____ Degree _____

Courses taken _____

_____

_____

_____

Special projects _____

_____

Dissertation (if applicable) _____

_____

Accomplishments _____

_____

Continuing education:

Course _____ Date _____

What it covered _____

_____

How did you apply this to your job or life? _____

_____

_____

_____

Course _____ Date _____

What it covered _____

_____

How did you apply this to your job or life? _____

_____

_____

Skills:

List applicable skills (e.g., typing, machine operations, computer, art, etc.) _TYPE, OPERATE A COPIER,_

_____

_____

Licenses, certifications, etc. (e.g., registered nurse, licensed electrician, member of bar, CPA, etc.) _____

_____

_____

_____

Job History

List in reverse chronological order. Include part-time and temporary work and military service if applicable.[4]

1. Title _____

   Company _____

   Dates: from _____ to _____

   Salary: starting _____ last _____

   Description of duties _____

   _____

_____

_____

_____

_____

What I liked about job _____

_____

_____

What I disliked _____

_____

_____

Accomplishments _____

_____

_____

_____

_____

Reason for leaving[5] _____

_____

2. Title _____

   Company _____

Dates: from _____ to _____

Salary: starting _____ last _____

Description of duties _____

_____

_____

_____

_____

_____

What I liked about job _____

_____

_____

What I disliked _____

_____

_____

Accomplishments _____

_____

_____

_____

_____

Reason for leaving[5] _____

_____

_____

3. Title _____

   Company _____

   Dates: from _____ to _____

   Salary: starting _____ last _____

   Description of duties _____

   _____

   _____

   _____

   _____

   What I liked about job _____

   _____

   _____

   What I disliked _____

   _____

   _____

Accomplishments _____

_____

_____

_____

_____

Reason for leaving[5] _____

_____

_____

4. Title _____

Company _____

Dates: from _____ to _____

Salary: starting _____ last _____

Description of duties _____

_____

_____

_____

_____

_____

What I liked about job _____

_____

_____

What I disliked _____

_____

_____

Accomplishments _____

_____

_____

_____

_____

Reason for leaving[5] _____

_____

_____

For additional jobs or assignments, use extra paper and insert with rest of questionnaire.

Volunteer Work*

1. Organization _____

   Time devoted: _____ hrs. per week

   Period of activity: from _____ to _____

*For persons who have devoted significant time in this area.

Description of duties _____

_____

_____

_____

_____

Comments[6] _____

_____

_____

_____

2. Organization _____

Time devoted: _____ hrs. per week

Period of activity: from _____ to _____

Description of duties _____

_____

_____

_____

_____

Comments[6] _____

_____

_____

Notes for P.B.O.

1. As the P.B.O. is designed to cover jobs of all types, many questions may not apply to you. Only answer those applicable to your background.

2. List only courses or activities different from the routine high school or college courses. (e.g., business courses, trade courses, leadership activities)

3. Indicate areas in school or outside activities which you feel were outstanding (e.g., honors, awards, especially satisfying part-time or summer jobs.)

4. If you have had several job assignments in the same company, list each as a separate job on the form. You will then be prepared to discuss the variety of your background and your progress in the company.

5. If your reason for leaving was a change of assignment within the same company, indicate if it was a transfer or a promotion and whether it was initiated by you or by the company.

6. List specific accomplishments such as money raised, ideas adopted, leadership roles, and any other relevant factors.

CHAPTER 3

PREPARING FOR THE INTERVIEW

Before every interview, it is to your advantage to review your P.B.O., with special attention to those aspects of your background that are pertinent to the job for which you are being considered. Remember that you should emphasize your strengths as they relate to each job and that jobs may differ depending upon the company, the department, and the situation. How to determine what a company desires will be covered later in this chapter.

Particular attention should be devoted to records of achievement. When you mention an achievement, the effect is enhanced if you can describe it clearly and easily. Hesitating, being vague on certain points, or groping for proper words destroys the effect you are trying to create. If you have sold more goods, developed a better manufacturing process, originated a better piece of advertising, or installed a better system or record-keeping method, be prepared to tell the interviewer about it in detail.

In short, be prepared to do yourself justice in the interview. Finding a job is a full-time occupation. To do it best, do it thoroughly by having adequate preparation.

Later in this book, we will list specific questions you might be asked in interviews for various types of jobs.

Preparing your answers to these will make your interview flow more smoothly and make you a more effective candidate.

Be prepared to answer detailed questions about your work. Specific information about equipment, methods, materials, and other phases of your work should be at your fingertips. Figures on sales volume, company size, budgets, and costs are data every person seeking management or administrative jobs should have set in their minds so they can be discussed fluently and intelligently. However, it is never necessary or advisable to divulge information considered confidential by your present or former employer. The interviewer will have more respect for you if you diplomatically indicate that certain matters are of a confidential nature.

If you are in a lower-ranking position, where such information is not known to you and probably not pertinent to your job, it will not be necessary for you to develop this type of data. However, you should be able to discuss your department, its function, and its place in the organization. Most important, you should be able to tell about your personal part in the department or the company's activities.

Recent high school or college graduates should be able to talk about their school grades, projects, extracurricular activities, and part-time or summer jobs. Indicate how your accomplishments in school demonstrated capability to learn, leadership, creativity, diligence, and other characteristics that may be important to success on the job for which you are applying.

The interviewer will want to know about your personal contributions to the successes of the activities in which you were engaged on previous jobs or in school. What did *you* do of particular merit—*your* production, *your* sales volume, *your* leadership roles, etc.

You are likely to be asked what you liked best and least about your job, as well as your reasons for leaving each job. If you thought this out when you prepared the P.B.O., your responses will reflect careful analysis of each situation rather than some off-the-cuff comment. Examples of good and poor responses to these questions will be given in the next chapter.

If your work is the type where samples of what you have done will demonstrate your achievements, preparation of a "presentation book" may be very effective. Such a book would include photographs of machines you have worked on or designed, merchandise displays you created, advertisements you have written. Also pertinent are charts showing your sales records, reports you have written, reports or projects completed on a job or in school, and related materials. The best way of presenting these items is to enclose each photo, chart, etc., in a clear plastic insert kept in a loose-leaf binder. During the interview, if a matter arises that can be illustrated by one of your charts or photos, show it at that time. Do not insist that the interviewer see your book. Use it as a salesperson would—at the right time to back up and strengthen something you are discussing.

OBTAIN INFORMATION ABOUT PROSPECTIVE EMPLOYERS

Alan J. asked one question of his interviewer that squashed any chance he had of getting the job, "What type of business is the J.J. Jones Co. in?" Mr. Jones, who had devoted all of his life to building up this business was appalled. How could anyone in his city not know about Jones's organization. Had Alan made the simplest inquiry, he would have not asked this embarrassing question. Most employers are proud of their companies and assume everybody knows who they are and what they do.

Marjorie G. fell into a different trap. She had worked for a very small company where all decisions were made by one person, the owner. When she went to Consolidated Industries for an interview, she assumed that she would see her prospective boss and after a brief interview would either be accepted or rejected. She made the appointment during her lunch hour. When she arrived at Consolidated, she was asked to fill out a detailed application form, take a typing test and then be interviewed by a personnel assistant. This took up her entire lunch hour plus. She had to beg off the next step—an interview with the office manager because she had no time. By the time she could return for the second interview, the company had already selected another applicant. Had Marjorie known the selection procedure, she would have given herself adequate time for all of it.

Before going on an interview, learn as much about the company, the job, and the interviewing procedure as possible. This is not always easy, but it is worth the trouble. The more you know about these factors, the more likely you are to avoid mistakes and present yourself as positively as possible.

LEARN ABOUT THE COMPANY

How much you need to know about the company depends on the level of the position for which you are applying. Persons seeking relatively low-level positions such as jobs in the plant or office in nonmanagerial capacities need much less information than candidates for higher level positions. Some of the things you should determine are the nature of the business (to avoid the faux pas Alan made), whether the company is large or small, and the approximate number of employees.

You will want to know if you are going to work as part of a large staff or just with one or two others. It is helpful to know in advance the physical setup of the office. Is it in a building by itself or in an office complex? You will feel more at ease when you get there if you are not surprised by the facility.

Another factor that would be helpful to determine is the reputation of the company in your area. Is it known as a good place to work? Does it have the reputation of keeping and promoting employees? What sort of training is it known to give? How stable is the company?

How can you find out these things? If you have been referred to this company by an employment agency, it should give you all of this information. If the agency does not volunteer the information you want, ask for it before accepting the referral. If you have been referred by a friend, ask him or her. If you have obtained the lead from an ad in the paper or from other indirect sources, you will have to research the company yourself.

Much of the information desired can be obtained by just asking around. You probably know somebody who either works, has worked, buys from, sells to, or in some other way knows the company. If this does not get you the needed data, telephone the company before you make your appointment and ask to speak to their public relations department. If there is no PR office, ask for sales or marketing and tell the respondent that you are seeking some information about the company. He or she will rarely ask why. Then ask a few very specific questions:

What is the nature of your business?
How long have you been in business?

How big is your sales volume?
How many employees do you have?
Where are you located?
What type of facility do you have?
What type of customers do you have (other businesses,
   direct consumers, government)?

If the company is large enough to be listed in a regional
or national directory of companies, you may obtain
some of the information by looking it up in the directory.
The major national directories include the following:

Dun and Bradstreet's Million Dollar Directory
Dun and Bradstreet's Middle Market Directory
Standard and Poor's Directory

In addition, there are special directories for many
industries such as banking, electronics, insurance, hotel,
and hospitals. Also, most states have statewide directories of manufacturing and other companies. These
directories will identify the nature of business of listed
companies and such additional information as sales
volume, number of employees, and the names of key
officers.

Most public libraries have a variety of directories in
their reference room. Ask the librarian to guide you to
the appropriate directory for the company you are
researching.

If you can obtain names of customers (particularly
other companies in your area), a call to the purchasing
agent of the customer can often enable you to obtain
additional information about the company and its reputation in the area.

Even if an employment agency did not refer you to the
job, if you have a contact in the agency (a counselor with
whom you have worked at one time is best), ask for
information about the company. Agencies can tell you a

good deal about the turnover of personnel in the company, the reports they get from former employees, and personnel policies and other important data.

Your high school or college placement office may have information about the company, so contact counselors and ask them what they know about it. Another good source of information is other companies in the same industry. Among your friends, relatives, or associates you are sure to find someone who can lead you to a person who can tell you something about the company.

For persons seeking positions in management, administration, or technical or professional categories, much more information is helpful. You will want to know specifics about sales volume, the profit picture, the company's growth history, its market share, and other details of its financial picture. You will also be interested in the type of management development programs the company offers and their record of management or administrative turnover. Any information you can learn about internal practices of the company as related to nepotism, demands on staff, etc., would be useful in determining how you should handle the interview or even if you want to apply at all. Some companies are known as tough places to work—places where the boss demands excessive hours of work or the sacrifice of all other aspects of one's life to the job.

In many jobs there are special problems. For example, if the company has facilities in other cities, you may be expected to move from time to time as part of your corporate growth. Some jobs entail considerable travel. All of these factors should be known to you before the interview, if possible, so you will not be faced with unexpected questions concerning them.

In addition to the sources previously discussed, managerial and related personnel should obtain more detailed information. If the company is a public company (i.e., stock is sold to the public either on a stock exchange or over the counter), annual reports are available to anybody interested—as required by the Securities Exchange Commission. You can get the annual report from the company itself or from a stockbroker.

Companies that are privately owned are not required to publish an annual report; however, information concerning their financial history and standing can be obtained by getting a Dun and Bradstreet report on them. Your bank can get this report for you at a reasonable cost.

The annual report or the Dun and Bradstreet report will usually give you details as to the company's profit picture, financial growth, sales volume, stability, and many other facts. If you do not know how to interpret these data, ask an accountant or business executive who is familiar with them to go over the report with you.

There are other financial services that analyze companies. Your banker or accountant can suggest those most appropriate for the company you are investigating.

LEARN ABOUT THE JOB

One of the advantages of being referred to a job by an employment agency is that it can give you a good idea of the nature of the job. However, if you do not have this advantage, it is still advisable to find out as much as you can about the nature of the job before the interview, so you can prepare your own strategy in adapting your background to the needs of that job.

Much of the key information needed concerns the duties and responsibilities of the position. If you learned about the job through an advertisement, review the ad carefully to determine the job's major duties from what is stated in the ad. However, this is not always possible because many ads are vague. It is not feasible to phone the interviewer in advance and ask for a copy of the job description, so if all you know about the job is the job title, you will have to depend on general knowledge of what that job usually entails.

Other factors you should try to determine are to whom the jobholder reports, what department the job is in, and the work hours. If the work schedule is different from usual work hours, requires frequent overtime, or requires working weekends or nights, it is good to know about it in advance.

If you have the opportunity to speak to people who work now or have previously worked in the company, try to learn about the working environment. Is it a fast-paced operation or a leisurely one? Is it a "friendly" place or a "businesslike" environment? Is it a small office or facility where everybody does everything or a large place where each person does a very specific job?

Learn what you can about the opportunity for advancement and the training offered, and it is good to have a fairly close estimate of the salary. These may be difficult to determine unless you are referred by an agency or somebody who has an intimate knowledge of the organization. It is not recommended that you try to get this directly from the company *before* the interview because most employers are reluctant to divulge this information until they are seriously interested in an applicant. However, if you do have indirect sources which can give this information to you before the interview, it will be another bit of help to you.

Candidates for higher-level jobs will want to have additional information about the job. They will find it helpful to see an organizational chart of the company and find out just where this job fits. Whom does it report to? Who reports to it? Where does the department fit into the entire organization? Organizational charts are not usually available to the public, but if an agency or executive recruiter has made the referral, they often know this.

Other questions senior people should try to uncover include the following: Why is the job open now? Is it a replacement or an expansion? If a replacement, what happened to the most recent holder of the job?

Management positions often require immediate or future relocation, heavy travel, or irregular hours. If you know about these things before the interview, it will be advantageous. There may be some unusual requirements for which you may not be prepared. A marketing manager thought he had a pretty good concept of what the job for which he was applying required. He prepared considerable data to show how he qualified but was completely surprised when he learned the job required foreign travel and a knowledge of European and South American markets. Had he known these requirements in advance, he could have elaborated further on his international background, which was not extensive, but adequate for the job.

LEARN ABOUT THE INTERVIEW SITUATION

You will recall the case of Marjorie G., who thought she could go through the selection procedure during her lunch hour. This problem can be avoided by asking one simple question when you make the appointment, "How much time should I allow for this appointment?" The secretary or receptionist will be happy to tell you. If possible, ask about other procedures that will be required, such as completing application forms, testing, and supplementary interviews.

In smaller companies there is often just one interview —with the person for whom the applicant will work. In larger organizations, the first interview is usually with a member of the personnel staff. This interview may be followed immediately or at a subsequent time by another interview—usually with the department head of the department where the vacancy exists. Persons applying for positions in higher levels of administration, management, or technical areas will often see several people before a final decision is made.

It is very important to know who makes the final decision on hiring. Ted L. prepared an excellent presentation for his interview and made a very strong impression on the personnel manager. However, when he was interviewed by the next executive, he answered many of his questions with the comment; "I told that to the personnel manager." By not realizing that the second interviewer was the decision maker, he lost out on the job. However, don't save all your ammunition for the decision maker. You must be just as effective with each person who interviews you because if any one of them is not impressed, you may never get to see the decision maker.

Sometimes you may not have the information needed to do your very best before the first interview, but in the case of multiple interviews, be sure to ask the very first interviewer all the questions necessary to give you full information about the company and the job before you go for your second round.

CHAPTER 4

INTERVIEW MANNERS

The concept that first impressions are lasting still holds true. There is an old saying in the field of personnel that hiring decisions are often made in the first thirty seconds of the interview, and the balance of the time is used to justify that decision. First impressions are almost always based on a reaction to your appearance. You cannot help whether you are tall or short, have sharp or soft features, blond or black hair, but you do have control over how you wear your hair, the clothes you choose, and your personal cleanliness and neatness.

Most readers of this book need not be reminded that clean fingernails, well-groomed hair, shined shoes, proper use of makeup, and other easily seen indicators of appearance are noted by the interviewer consciously or subconsciously immediately upon meeting you. A careful check of these items should be made before going on an interview.

What clothes should you wear? Books have been written on how one should dress for success. Some of the suggestions in these books are applicable for job seekers. A simple rule to follow, however, is that it is usually best to be conservative in choosing what to wear at a job interview. Unusual clothes draw attention to the clothes, not to the person. If you dress in too casual a fashion, it may be interpreted that you are casual about your work. In selecting your wardrobe for the interview keep in mind the type of job for which you are applying and the type of person who is likely to interview you. If it is at all possible, visit the company before the interview day and note what most people are wearing. If you notice that the women all wear dresses, it would be unwise for you to wear slacks. If the men all wear sports jackets and coordinated slacks, you would be in line if you wore the same type of outfit at the interview. However, most people do not have this opportunity, so you will be safer to wear the more conservative style—a dress or tailored suit for a woman and a suit for a man. In some occupations and professions, more casual wear is expected. Engineers are more likely to be seen in sports outfits than bankers or accountants; sales people who call on plant managers or travel to midwestern, western, or southern territories usually dress more casually than those calling on the Eastern Establishment or international customers.

Just as clothes should be chosen with care, the hairstyle one wears should be congruent with what is accepted in the type of job for which one is applying. Far-out coiffures and trendy hairstyles are more likely to cause negative reactions. Long hair for men—even when neatly groomed—will turn off older interviewers.

Although more and more executives are wearing beards, there is still a good deal of prejudice against beards in many companies. It is not suggested that all job applicants shave off their beards, but it must be understood that beards may not be an asset. Today, mustaches are generally accepted in most organizations.

Both men and women are cautioned not to wear strong perfumes or colognes. Light fragrances are much more appropriate in a business setting.

Be on time! Nothing makes as poor an impression on an interviewer as a late applicant. If you are not familiar with the location, make a trial run sometime before the interview. Give yourself extra time in case of traffic problems. Arrive at the reception area about ten minutes before the appointed time. You may be required to complete an application form before the interview.

In filling out applications (whether at home if mailed to you or at the personnel office), always follow instructions carefully. Some companies require that the application be filled out in your own handwriting; others ask for it to be done in pen or pencil and not typed. Make sure you answer all the questions as completely as space allows. Never write "see resume" in answer to a question. Even worse is to not answer any questions, but just scrawl over the entire application "see resume." Companies ask you to complete their form because they want the information asked on it, not what you have on your resume. They also want a standard form completed so that applicants can be more easily compared. It is true that most application forms do not provide adequate space for details of experience. Fill it out as best you can and then indicate that your resume is attached to give the interviewer supplemental information. The resume should be considered just that—a supplement, not a substitute for the application form.

In most instances, the interviewer will come out to the reception area to greet you and invite you into his or her office. Occasionally the applicant is ushered into the interviewer's office by a secretary. In either case it is appropriate to shake hands with the interviewer. Both men and women should have a firm but not bone-crushing handshake. Look at the interviewer and acknowledge his or her greeting. Do not sit down until invited to do so. Sometimes you will be interviewed by more than one person. The principal interviewer will introduce you to the others. Shake hands with each and repeat their names so you will be sure to remember them.

INTERVIEWER: Mr. Applicant, meet Ms. Taylor, who is our Director of Marketing.
APPLICANT: Glad to have the opportunity of meeting you, Ms. Taylor.

Unless you are being interviewed for a job with a tobacco company, do not ask to smoke at the interview. Unless the interviewer smokes and invites you to smoke, do not light up. Even if you are told you may smoke if you like, do not smoke unless the interviewer is also smoking. If you are not a smoker and the interviewer does smoke, when asked if you would like to smoke, it is not necessary to make a speech about your feelings about smoking. Just decline politely.

During the interview sit comfortably in your chair. Watch for signs of nervousness that often occur among applicants. If you start playing with your eyeglasses, your handbag, your pen or pencil, stop! Do not cross and uncross your legs. Avoid shaking or nodding your head in response to questions or comments. Be sure that you do not place your hand in front of your mouth. This gesture is not only a nervous habit, but it makes it difficult to hear what you are saying. Speak clearly—not too loudly but not so softly that one has to strain to hear you.

Much has been said about maintaining eye contact with the interviewer. This advice has been often misunderstood. Have you ever had a conversation with anyone whose eyes never left yours during the entire conversation? It is very distracting and often annoying.

Don't stare at the interviewer, yet always look at him or her. Look at the entire person, not just at his or her eyes. Your eyes should focus on various parts of the interviewer's face at various times during the interview. Don't look out the window or at a picture on the wall. Keep your attention on the interviewer. If more than one person is interviewing you, look primarily at the person who asked you the question you are answering, but from time to time also turn to the others when making a point.

The most important key to interview behavior is to *listen!* Pick up the nuances in what the interviewer is saying. You can hear these by the inflections and tonal variations. Matters which are important to him or her will be expressed in stronger tones than will lesser matters. Respond to every question. Often, applicants are so anxious to tell their stories that they do not listen carefully to the questions and give a response that is not related to what the interviewer has asked.

CHAPTER 5

QUESTIONS YOU CAN EXPECT TO BE ASKED

Most interviewers, to make you feel at ease, will start the interview by talking about matters of a trivial or noncontroversial nature. They may talk about the weather, ask you if you had any difficulty getting to the plant or office, comment about sporting events, etc. As soon as the interviewer feels you are comfortable in the situation, he or she will begin asking questions about your background. Most interviewers talk about each phase of your education and experience separately. Some prefer to begin with questions on education and training; others start with questions about your most recent job. Be prepared to talk in detail about each of the positions you have held, particularly your current or last job.

An overview question to get a general picture of your background is often used as the first significant inquiry. *Tell me about a typical day on your job.* Or, *Describe your duties and responsibilities on your last job.* It is important that you be prepared to tell the interviewer what you did in a manner that will reflect your strongest points. The interviewer will use the answer to the overview question as the basis for the balance of the interview. If you have any special strengths you wish to emphasize, mention them early in your answer. For example, if your strong point is the technical aspect of the job, but you are less qualified in the administrative functions, in answering the overview question, play up the technical phases. Interviewers tend to concentrate on the factors brought up by the applicant.

Part of the interview will focus on your job experience and training for the position you are applying for. Other questions will be asked on personal factors. Let's first look at some of the types of job-oriented questions you might expect.

Discuss some of the problems you encountered on the job. Tell about those you solved, not those you could not handle.

How did you change the content of your job from when you assumed it until now? The purpose of this question is to see how much creativity and initiative you have. Most jobs, other than highly structured routine ones, allow for flexibility on the part of the jobholder. Give some examples of how you took on added responsibilities, improved systems or procedures, made the job more effective, etc.

What do you consider to be your chief accomplishment in each of the jobs you have held? Prepare specific examples of these accomplishments. To make your answer even more effective, tell what the situation was that you faced and how you handled it. If the result of your work can be measured in terms of dollars earned, profits made, losses prevented, etc., bring out this point.

What in your background particularly qualifies you to do the job? Point out past experience in similar work, special education, training that is pertinent, or skills you possess that will be useful in this job. If you have not had experience that is directly related to the open position, play up your ability to learn rapidly. Give examples of how, in previous assignments, you took over work with which you had little or no experience and rapidly became productive.

A variation on the preceding question is, *In what way has your education and training prepared you for this job?* If you have specific education in the field, this question is easy to answer. However, if your education is only tangential to the field, break down the components of the job (e.g., communication skills, analytical skills) and show how your education prepared you in these areas.

What disappointments did you have in your previous jobs? The objective of this question is to see how you handled failures and unmet aspirations. Most people face some failures in many aspects of their lives. There is nothing to be ashamed about in admitting failures or disappointments. In discussing failures do not place the blame on others. Tell how you coped with the particular failure. For example, "I worked for six months trying to obtain a contract from the XYZ Company. The purchasing agent and the chief engineer assured me I would get the contract, but the president vetoed it. I analyzed every step I took in these negotiations and I guess I didn't realize the president's concern with one aspect of our deal. I never made that mistake again."

In what areas did you need help and guidance from your boss? Point out how you used the boss' guidance to help you grow and that you requested help only in unusual situations.

For what things have your superiors complimented you? Here is your chance to blow your horn. Tell about your special commendations, awards, accomplishments. Also include the day-to-day compliments you received even if they were not for outstanding work. You might say, "My boss always told me how dependable I was," or "He could always count on me when things got tight." This question is always a prelude to the next one; *For what things did your boss criticize you?* Try to have one or two relatively innocuous matters ready in answer to this question. The best approach to answering this type of question is to pick some aspect of the former job that is not needed in the one for which you are applying and comment on that as an area of criticism.

Of all the aspects of your last job, what did you like best? like least? These must be treated much like the question just discussed. To make a favorable impression on the interviewer, select aspects of your jobs most closely related to the open position as your most enjoyable factors and those less closely related as the ones liked least. If this job requires considerable work in areas *not* liked by you, it would be advisable to withdraw from consideration for the job. You would probably be unhappy in it.

When asked questions such as, *What are your strengths? your weaknesses? What can you contribute to this job? What aspects of the job that is open do you feel least qualified to do?*, always keep in mind the job for which you are being interviewed and talk about your strengths and qualifications that are most appropriate to this job. When asked about negative aspects of your background, talk about those which are not important for this job.

In addition to these general questions you will be asked very specific questions about every aspect of the jobs and education you have had. In the next chapter of this book you will find examples of such specific questions for a wide variety of job categories. Study carefully those that are closest to your field of work before going on any interview.

Questions to determine your attitudes, motivation, resourcefulness, character, stability, etc., will also be interspersed throughout an interview. *What are you seeking in this job that you are not getting in your present job?* Before answering this question be sure the job can offer you what you want. If you answer "A lot of money" and the job will pay only a modest salary, you might knock yourself out of consideration. "Opportunity for growth and advancement" is usually a good answer but would be unsatisfactory if the job is in one of the many job categories where you might have job security, a decent salary, but little chance for advancement. Look into the job and make sure it does meet your real goals before considering it as a career opportunity.

What is your long-term objective? Be realistic. If you want to become a manager and this job is three steps below management but has long-range possibility, tell the interviewer that management is your goal but also say that you know you have to pay your dues before you earn the right to a management position. Be prepared to answer the follow-up question, *What are you planning to do to meet this objective?* Tell about special training you are taking or planning to take, what you desire to learn on the job, and any other plans you have to acquire the skills needed.

A variation on the preceding question is, *Where do you expect to be in five (ten) years?* Some applicants think that by replying "A high position," they will show ambition. This answer may show foolishness. The implication of "I want *your* job" or "I expect to be a vice-president" had better be backed up with some plan to get to that position—not just a wish. It is better to answer such a question with, "Depending on the opportunities available to me, I want to move as far as I can in my field."

What were the reasons for leaving each of your previous jobs? Give the true reasons, of course. If elaboration is needed, explain the reasons in more detail. If the cause of termination is not positive, describe the circumstances frankly. "I couldn't get along with my boss. He was very demanding and often screamed at me. I took it for six months—and that was longer than any of the previous secretaries he had had over the past several years."

Why are you seeking a job now? The key word is "now." If you are currently employed, tell why you made the decision to look for a new job at this time rather than at an earlier or later date.

What were your original career goals? How have they changed over the years? If you have changed career goals, tell how your career has progressed and what precipitated changes, what you did to implement these changes, and how they affected your progress.

Describe your supervisor's supervisory methods. If you have worked under several supervisors, compare their management approaches. Specify the ones with whom you worked best and those with whom you had difficulty.

In your previous jobs how much of your work was done on your own and how much as part of a team? The interviewer wants to see if you are a loner or a team person. Tell what committees you served on and what part you played in that group's work, what team projects you worked on, how you worked in cooperation with others in your department and with other departments.

Another type of question often used by interviewers is the "situational" question. A hypothetical situation is posed and you are asked to tell how you would handle it. These matters generally are ones that would occur on the job for which you are applying. Give careful thought to the question before answering. An off-the-cuff response could be ill advised. Some examples of these situational questions include the following:

> SECRETARY: *Your boss is in an important conference and cannot be disturbed. A good customer comes in unannounced and demands to see your boss. How would you handle this?*

A good response might be; "I'd explain the situation to the customer and tell him when the conference was scheduled to end. I'd ask him if anyone else could handle his problem and make every effort to see that he received some attention from someone in authority if he was unable or unwilling to wait or come back."

> SALESPERSON: *A customer phones and is irate. The merchandise promised for delivery that morning did not arrive. His entire production line is backed up waiting for the material.*

A good response might be, "I'd calm him down by admitting it is a serious problem and tell him that I would immediately investigate the situation and find out the status of the order. If there was any way to get the material to his plant that day, I'd do all I could, even if I had to stop everything else I was doing to accomplish it. I'd follow through and get to him as soon as I had some information."

Probably the most confusing type of question to many applicants is the "nondirective" question. Here the interviewer throws the ball to the applicant and allows him or her to talk without guidance. The objective is to give the applicant the chance to tell things that might not be thought of by the interviewer. Nondirective questions may come at the beginning of the interview or at any time during the interview.

The most frequent nondirective opener is, *Tell me about yourself.* In answering this question, you have the opportunity of really selling yourself or knocking yourself out of contention. Always be prepared for such a question. Outline your strong points and describe them in detail point by point. Many people start their response to this question by telling about their childhood, early education, family life, etc. This approach weakens the presentation. Concentrate on job accomplishments. If the interviewer wants to know about those other aspects, it will come out later in the interview.

Other nondirective questions include open-ended questions about phases of your background. *Tell me about . . .* is the usual opener of a nondirective question. The interviewer will usually not interrupt, but if you stop talking, he or she will either remain silent or make a nonmeaningful sound such as "yes," "uh-huh," or "mmmmm." You must keep talking. Many an applicant has told about matters that should never be brought out because he or she did not know how to control this type of questioning.

In the following example, the applicant is a woman seeking a supervisory position:

INTERVIEWER: Tell me about your supervisory experi-
   ence.
APPLICANT: I supervised eight people.
INTERVIEWER: (silence)
APPLICANT: Five of them were women; three were men.
INTERVIEWER: Yes
APPLICANT: I had no trouble with the women, but had a
   difficult time supervising those men.

Had the applicant understood that one must carefully think out the responses to such nondirective questions, she would have emphasized a strength about her supervisory experience, rather than uncovering a weakness.

By knowing the types of questions you are likely to be asked and by carefully evaluating your background in relation to the job for which you are applying, you will be better prepared to give answers that will reflect your advantages and minimize your limitations for the job. Rehearsing questions and answers with a knowledgable person in your field will help you make a more effective presentation and will immeasurably improve your chances of obtaining the job.

CHAPTER **6**

QUESTIONS RELATED TO SPECIFIC JOB CATEGORIES

Each person applying for a job in a specific job category should expect to be quizzed in detail about that type of work. You should review your own work background with particular attention to the technical and specialized aspects of the jobs you have held, and you should be prepared to answer all kinds of questions about them.

Most important—answer each question with details about *your own* experience and accomplishments in that work, rather than making vague generalizations. Tie in what you have done and how it succeeded in meeting company objectives, instead of giving a theoretical discourse on the subject. For example, if you are a personnel specialist and are asked about job evaluation, rather than answering with an academic analysis of various job evaluation systems, tell just what you did in evaluating jobs in your previous positions. If you have had little or no experience, then you can tell about the courses you have taken and indicate that you are able to apply this knowledge.

On the following pages are specific questions to be expected for a large variety of job titles. Read those questions that are closest to your own experience and prepare to answer them at your interviews. If your specialty is not included, by studying related areas you can obtain a good idea of the types of questions you may face. Using these questions from related areas as a guide, work out a list of questions that might be asked based on your knowledge of the field and prepare responses to them.

Accountant

For what accounting activities were you responsible?

In answering this question, be sure to give a clear picture of the nature of your activities. If you had specific responsibility for such things as budgets, financial analysis, or taxes, identify them. If you were primarily responsible for keeping journals and ledgers, indicate what types of journals and ledgers they were and your other functions such as accounts payable, accounts receivable, preparing schedules, payrolls, trial balances, profit and loss statements, balance sheets, annual reports.

What auditing experience have you had?

If this experience was with a CPA (certified public accounting) firm, discuss the types of clients serviced and the problems faced. If you were an internal auditor, indicate the level of your responsibility.

Describe some of the systems and controls you developed.

Systems and procedures often involve analysis of paper flow. Describe in detail the specific forms you designed and tell how they solved the problem. What systems did you establish that did not involve new forms?

In what tax jurisdictions have you had experience?

Specify whether your experience has been just with the federal government or if it involved specific state or municipal taxes. If you have foreign tax experience, be sure to mention it.

Other than income taxes, what tax returns have you prepared?

If you have been involved with the preparation of returns or statements for sales taxes, excise taxes, or other types of taxes, this is the time to discuss it.

How large a volume of tax returns did you handle?

The quantity of your tax activity may be important.

With what types of cost systems are you familiar?

Cost accounting experience varies with the type of industry in which the cost accountant works. In preparation for your interview, you should determine the nature of the industry and whether it is likely to use standard costs, process costs, or job costs. If your experience or training has prepared you for this type of cost accounting, emphasize this fact at the interview. If not, you will have to convince the employer that you can learn the company's methods rapidly.

What experience have you had in setting up incentive systems?

For what types of work have these incentive systems been established? Was it a simple piecework system or a more complex one?

Describe your experience with labor costs.

Indicate what you did to determine direct and indirect labor costs.

What types of forecasting did you prepare?

Be specific as to the type of forecast (market studies, long-range business forecasts, production planning, etc.) and the part you played in preparing the forecast. Be prepared to discuss how accurate your forecasts were compared with actual results.

What other types of financial analysis did you do?

Talk about your work in risk analysis, mergers and acquisitions, inventory management, information reporting, etc.

What background do you have with budgets?

Tell the interviewer what types of budgets you worked on, such as general budgets, departmental budgets, capital budgets. Discuss your part in preparing the budget or analyzing budgets.

What exposure have you had to computers?

Most accountants today have some knowledge of data processing. You need not be a programmer or computer specialist. Play up whatever contact you have had in data processing, including interfacing with the computer people in your previous jobs, preparing accounting material for the computer, working with computer output. If you have taken any courses in data processing, be sure to mention them.

Advertising

Although a large percentage of advertising writing is done by professional ad agencies, most companies do have advertising departments which work closely with the agency and often do a portion of the creative work themselves. The most common assignments of the internal advertising department are setting advertising policy, coordinating the marketing department of the company with the agency's staff, and making major advertising decisions based on the agency's recommendations. Where no agency is involved, all of this activity falls in the advertising department's jurisdiction. Whether your experience is with an agency or a company, the following questions are likely to be asked.

Describe the sales promotional material for which you were responsible.

Before going to interviews, prepare copies of some of the best material you have written. Be able to talk about how they were designed, what part you played compared with others in your agency or company, and, if known, what the results of the promotion were.

What responsibility did you have for art and layout?

If you did the art work, the work itself will tell the whole story. If you directed artists by giving them ideas or instructions, describe what you did.

Describe or show some of the ads you wrote.

In explaining the ad copy, discuss the objectives of the ad, what problems you had in choosing the approach taken, what part you played in the decision, and how the final copy met the objectives. Some measurements of the ad's results helps immeasurably.

What other aspects of advertising and sales promotion did you handle?

Describe your other functions such as marketing studies, preparation of direct mail campaigns, working with sales people, handling cooperative advertising, etc.

For what advertising decisions were you responsible?

If you were in a management position, here is your chance to tell about your accomplishments as a decision maker. If not, tell what you did to assist management in making final decisions on advertising or related areas.

With what media have you worked?

If you are strong in radio or TV, tell the interviewer some of the stations and programs with which you worked. Discuss your part in choosing the media and writing or approving the commercials or the programs themselves. If your forte is print media, indicate the magazines or newspapers with which you worked and, of course, display some of your ads. If your background is in brochures or other types of promotional material, examples and discussions of the backgrounds of each piece make the best presentation.

Tell me about your background in packaging, displays, or other advertising material.

In many companies, these functions are even more significant than copywriting or media ads. Photographs of point-of-purchase displays and samples of packages you have designed should be in your portfolio. If you did not design them, discuss your part in purchasing them and working with the creators.

Describe your relationship with the marketing activity of the company.

If you worked under the jurisdiction of the marketing manager, discuss how your function meshed with his or hers. Tell what you did in market research (either directly or indirectly), new-product analysis, etc. If you were in technical, financial, or other specialized fields, be sure to display your knowledge of that field by using the jargon associated with that kind of work. Use of occasional technical terminology convinces people in that area that you "belong."

Auditor

Whether your experience has been with a CPA firm or as an internal auditor, the following questions may be asked. Naturally, your responses will differ somewhat depending upon where you had your auditing experience.

What types of clients (or departments) did you audit?

Tell the nature of the businesses involved, the size of the client, department or division, the role you played in the audit (were you in charge of it or part of a team?), and other pertinent information that will help the interviewer understand just what you have done.

Tell me about some of the problems you uncovered in your audits.

Most auditing work is routine, but it is the special problems that are uncovered that make the auditor worth his or her salary. Prepare several examples of how you saved your company money, uncovered deviations from proper accounting methods, or, more dramatic, discovered frauds or unraveled complex situations.

How did you present your findings to the management?

If you had direct access to top management, discuss how this was done. If you had to go through channels, tell about the procedure. Were your reports made verbally? In a formal manner?

To whom did you report?

The rank and position of your boss often reflects on you.

What responsibility did you have for auditing outside contractors, vendors, subcontractors, etc.?

53

The more diversified your background, the better you appear. Any work you did in auditing outside organizations should be mentioned even if it was minor.

What was your relationship to your employer's CPA firm?

This question is obviously designed for internal auditors. Tell who the CPA firm was and what interface you had with this firm.

If you also conducted management audits, describe the purpose of these audits and how you went about them.

Management audits require the ability to understand much more about an operation than just the accounting aspects. The management auditor is often involved in evaluating systems and procedures, examining operations and productivity, and recommending major changes. The management auditor is like an internal consultant and should have a considerable knowledge of the business. If you have this type of background it may be extremely valuable to the employer.

How much travel did your job entail?

Travel is essential in many auditing jobs. If possible, determine before the interview if the job requires travel so you will be prepared to answer honestly about your willingness to travel as much as required. Try never to let the need for extensive travel be a surprise to you at the interview. If you are aware that the job calls for more travel than you are willing to do, decline the invitation for the interview so that you do not waste your time or the employer's.

What courses or seminars have you taken this year?

*To what professional associations do you belong?
What part do you play in those associations' activities?*

Auditors, like all professional people, should keep up with the state of the art in their fields. Tell about specific courses and seminars you attended and how you applied what you learned to your work.

What experience have you had with the computer?

Computers are now part of almost every job. Whatever experience you have in this area will be helpful.

What other responsibilities did you have with your previous employers?

If your work involved other accounting or management functions, describe them. Background in financial analysis, budgets, systems, and procedures can be assets. On the other hand, if too much of your time was devoted to these other areas it may weaken your experience for a full-time auditor's position.

Bookkeeper or Accounting Clerk

In your previous experience, for what accounting functions were you responsible?

This question is geared to find out your general background, so be prepared to describe the major areas of your work such as keeping journals and ledgers, handling payrolls, running balances, etc. Remember that the interviewer will take each item you mention in answering this question and probe you for your knowledge and competence in that area. So if you are particularly strong in certain phases of the job, stress them in your response.

What books did you keep?

If you kept a full set of books, say so and then elaborate further. If you only handled special accounts, such as accounts payable or accounts receivable, indicate this fact.

To what stage did you handle the books?

Did you carry the books through the trial balance? Did you prepare final statements for the CPA's approval?

To whom did you report?

Did you report to the office manager? an officer of the company? the controller? another bookkeeper?

What responsibility have you had for payroll? Describe the payroll system.

Tell how large a payroll it was. Discuss your experience in computing commissions for sales people, incentives for productivity, overtime. Did you use any special type of payroll system or equipment?

What responsibility did you have for handling cash?

How much cash? How did you keep accounts on cash?

What tax returns did you handle?

If you compiled the monthly or quarterly payroll taxes, withholding taxes, federal or state income taxes, sales taxes, etc., be prepared to discuss your part. If you did all the work and the CPA only approved it, make sure this fact is stated.

What was your responsibility for handling accounts payable?

Tell about the volume of payables. Describe your company's procedure for processing an invoice from receipt of the bill until it is paid. You might expand on any special systems your company used to assure bills were correct and discounts taken.

What was your responsibility for handling accounts receivable?

Tell how you kept track of money due the company, how you aged accounts, what you did to collect delinquent accounts if that was part of your duties, and what part you played (if any) in the credit-collection procedure of your company.

Which accounting machines have you operated?

Mention any experience or training you might have on any of the standard bookkeeping machines, calculators, billing machines, or, of course, computers.

Computer Operations
KEYPUNCH OPERATOR

What model machines have you operated?

Specify the manufacturer and model number.

What is your keypunch speed?

You may be asked to take a test to verify this.

Did you verify your work?

If so, tell by what means it was verified. If not, indicate who verified it and if you verified the work of other operators.

With what other equipment are you familiar?

If you have background in other peripheral equipment, such as optical scanners, it will be an asset.

Who scheduled your work?

If you scheduled your own work, tell how you prepared the schedule.

What was your average daily work load?

Work loads vary depending upon the type of work done, the type of equipment used, and the needs of the company. Some work is regular. You are busy all the time and work at a steady pace. In other operations, the work comes in spurts. You may be rushed much of the time, but have periods where there is little to do. If you have worked under pressure, be sure to tell the interviewer. If you do not like to work under pressure and the job will call for this, it may be wise to withdraw from consideration.

What was the nature of the work you did?

Tell whether your work was primarily sales data,

technical data, personnel figures, inventory, etc. The more detail you can give the employer, the more likely you are to make a favorable impression.

COMPUTER OPERATOR

With what equipment are you experienced?

This is a key question. Tell about *all* the equipment on which you worked, including both mainframe and peripheral.

What experience do you have with tape? discs? Which types?

Be specific in your response.

With what auxiliary equipment are you familiar?

If you have not mentioned this information in your answer to the first question, specify what background you have both on the job and in training with each of the units you know.

Where did you learn to operate this equipment?

Did you obtain your training in school, on the job, in the military? If your training was with a computer manufacturer (e.g., IBM, Burroughs), this fact should be brought out. If the employer uses the equipment of that manufacturer, it is an advantage. Even if the employer uses other equipment, training by any manufacturer is nevertheless helpful.

Have you been involved with coding? programming? tape or disc libraries?

Some operators are exposed to these and other areas of the EDP (electronic data processing) department in their work. The more knowledge you have about data processing, the more value you will be to the employer. Even if the current position does not call for the skills you have, they will be noted for consideration in the future. Companies prefer people who have potential for growth.

What type of work load did you handle?

See comments for the sixth question for keypunch operator.

What was the nature of the work you did?

See comments for the seventh question for keypunch operator.

Credit and Collection Specialist

What types of customers did you evaluate for credit?

Were they industrial companies, retail stores, consumers? Find out in advance the types of customers the employers deals with. If you have not dealt with similar customers, prepare to show the similarities in handling your type of customers and those the employer deals with.

Describe what steps you took from the inception of the credit evaluation until the final decision was reached.

This will give the employer an overview of your duties, so be sure to cover all steps.

What criteria did you use to reach the credit decision?

Your judgment in making credit decisions is the chief asset you offer. Give specific examples of how you decided to give or reject credit and the bases for these decisions.

What factors influenced you most in a customer's financial statement?

Tell about the ratios you analyzed, the weight you gave to tangible assets versus goodwill, growth record, etc.

What sources did you use in checking a customer?

Indicate the credit-reporting services you used, such as Dun and Bradstreet. If you checked banks or other credit references, tell how you accomplished this and be prepared to give details.

61

What has your experience been in using credit-investigating services?

What services? Discuss how you used this information. What weight was it given in relation to other sources of information? If you had either very good or very bad experiences in using these sources, give examples.

Who made the final credit decision? Who had the last word?

If you did not make the final decision, who did? What was your part in the decision? Tell whether you made recommendations which were then acted upon by your boss or whether you just presented the facts and the boss made the decision.

Tell me, how did you handle pressures from salespeople when the customer's credit was in doubt? when it was rejected?

Salespeople often pressure credit specialists to be more liberal than they should be. If you have had such an experience, tell how you handled it and give examples of both standing firm when it was indicated and being flexible when that was the best course.

A salesperson lands an account he or she has been pursuing for several months. Your credit reports show a history of slow payments and occasional litigation. What do you do?

This is called a situational question (see chapter 5). Think carefully before answering. If you have actually faced a similar situation, describe what you did. If not, a good answer would show flexibility and diplomacy. One possible response: "I would check further to see if the slow payments were made within reasonable periods of time or if litigation was necessary. If credit checks indicated a good current financial position, and the slow payments were some time ago and recent experience was better, I would approve the credit. If payments were still very slow, I might suggest a method of payment by schedules that would fit the customer's capability."

What was the standard operating procedure for collections in your company?

The earlier questions related to credit; now the emphasis is on collections. This is another overview question, and as in most overview questions, the objective is to get a general picture of this phase of your background and from your responses expand to specific questions. In preparing for the interview, review your procedures carefully, so that you can talk about them with ease and be able to answer any questions asked about specific details.

Tell me about some of your more difficult collection problems.

Emphasize those in which you collected the full amount due by creative means. If the interviewer asks about some of your failures, do not be ashamed to admit them. No credit or collection specialist wins them all.

How did you handle the really good customer who is overextended and paying slowly?

Give examples of how you saved a customer for the company by rescheduling payments and working with the customer to get full payment without resorting to litigation.

What was the loss ratio of your company in each of the past several years?

If your loss ratio is high, it is difficult to justify it unless you come from an industry in which loss ratios are usually high. (Companies selling to consumers [i.e., furniture, appliances] have a higher loss ratio than industrial companies.) If the latter case applies to you, be sure to bring out this fact and, if true, show how your company's losses were less than others in the same industry. Another factor that might mitigate a high loss ratio is if you have reduced the losses after taking over the job from your predecessor.

What collection techniques worked best for you?

Here is your chance to tell of your expertise in writing collection letters, using the telephone as a collection tool, enlisting the assistance of the sales force, or adopting whatever approach you preferred.

At what point do you turn over an account to a collection agency?

Collection agencies should be used only as a last resort. However, if you did use these agencies, discuss at what point you referred the account, how you assisted the agency so it could do the best job for you, which agencies you used, and your record of success with them.

Clerk-Typist

Applicants for typist jobs or any job involving typing must be prepared to take typing tests to determine speed and accuracy. If you have not taken a typing test for some time, it is a good idea to practice for it by timing your typing speed. Most typing exercise books (available in paperback bookstores or in your library) have such tests in them. For jobs involving considerable typing, a minimum speed of fifty words per minute is usually required. The faster you type, the more likely you are of obtaining the job. Accuracy is also important, and the typing test usually has standards for the number of acceptable errors.

What kind of typewriters have you used?

Almost all offices today use electric typewriters. Some of them are designed for special purposes and require training in their use. Memory, IBM executive, and some other typewriters are in particular demand. If you have not had experience with any machine that is required on the job, indicate your willingness to learn how to use the machine.

What sort of material did you type?

Did you type special documents, invoices, statistical tables? Did you fill out forms? write letters?

How would you set up a letter?

Letters can be set up in several ways. If asked this question, state that you know that each company has its own style of writing a letter, but the one you have used is the one you will outline. Then take a piece of paper and outline a typical letter. For example:

                                           Date
Name of Person
Name of Company
Address
City, State, Zip

Dear Sir:

                                    Sincerely,
                                    Name of Company

                                    John J. Jones
                                    Vice-President

An inquiry comes from a customer about an out-of-stock item. A new supply is expected in about a month. Write a letter answering the inquiry.

This is a situational question (see chapter 5). The objective is to determine how you handle problems of this sort. Think carefully before you answer such a question and then be sure to set up a letter that is clear, concise, and diplomatic.

A good response:

                                         July 1, 1981

Mr. W. S. Gilbert
Gilbert & Sullivan, Inc.
29 Doyle St.
New York, NY 10002

Dear Mr. Gilbert:
  The valves about which you inquired (Catalog #345) are temporarily out of stock. We expect a shipment in about thirty days and will be able to deliver them to you immediately upon receiving them in our warehouse.

We regret the delay in filling your order and thank you for your patience.

Sincerely,
Variable Valves, Inc.

Frank Franklin
Sales Manager

FF:bb

Have you typed from dictating equipment?

Indicate what types of dictating equipment you used and what percentage of your work involved using such equipment. If you do not have such experience, indicate a willingness to learn.

How did you spend the rest of the time on the job?

This question will give you a chance to tell about all of the other duties you performed in addition to typing. If you kept records, worked with figures or statistics, wrote reports, or checked the work of others, make sure the employer learns about it now.

Tell me about some of the special assignments on which you worked in your previous jobs.

If you worked in an insurance department, mention the work you did processing claims or applications for insurance. If you worked in a sales office, talk about sales reports, commission calculations, customer service, or whatever else you did that was different from the job of a typical clerk-typist.

What experience have you had in word processing?

As word processing is the fastest-growing area in office work, most typists will have to become acquainted with it sooner or later. If you have worked any of the word-processing equipment, it will be an asset. If not, don't be concerned. Tell the employer that you are very interested in learning to operate this new type of equipment, and inasmuch as you are a good typist (if true), you should master it readily.

Electronics Engineer

What products or equipment did you design?

Be prepared to discuss the various components, equipment, or other material you worked on. If feasible, bring samples, photographs, drawings, or blueprints to illustrate your work.

With what types of circuits have you worked?

Show how you worked with analog, digital, integrated circuits, printed circuits, etc.

With what equipment have you worked in your R&D (research and development) activities?

Discuss any sophisticated equipment used.

Describe some of your work by telling what you did from the conception of the design through the manufacture and testing of the finished product.

Many engineers have only worked on phases of a project. However, if you have had this comprehensive experience, it should be discussed in detail. If you only worked on certain aspects, tell about the entire project and explain the specific part you took.

What experience have you had in packaging components into systems?

Tell what kinds of components and what kinds of systems were involved.

What experience have you had with military specifications?

As so much of electronics work is related to the military, knowledge of "milspecs" is useful.

Tell me about some of the unusual technical problems you faced and how you handled them.

This will give you the chance to show your creativity, innovation, and knowledge of your field. Prepare several such examples before going on interviews.

What management responsibilities did you have?

Tell about your administrative and other nontechnical duties and how they contributed to your department's success.

How many people did you supervise? What job categories?

Draw an organizational chart of your department and tell what each of your subordinates did.

What authority did you have for purchasing equipment?

Tell what equipment you bought, what steps you took to assure that it was the best-suited equipment, what responsibility you had for negotiating price, etc.

Describe some of the technical material you had to write.

This would include such things as instructions to users, manuals, catalogs, brochures about the products, etc. If samples are available, bring them along to illustrate your work.

Tell about your experience in interfacing with the sales and marketing departments to determine their technological needs or to provide technical assistance in selling the product.

Give specific instances of where your help was of value.

What experience have you had in customer relations?

Tell about how you handled customers' complaints and inquiries or how you evaluated customers' needs.

In addition to the preceding questions, be prepared to answer very technical questions in your field. These will usually not be asked by the personnel department, but by the department head of the department where the job exists.

Factory Supervisor

Questions for factory supervisors are usually divided among the functions of the job.

PRODUCTION PLANNING

What responsibility did you have for planning your day's production? for longer-range (weekly or more) production?

Some supervisors are required to do their own short-term planning, with specialists doing the long-range planning. Others do both or neither. Tell what part you had in making production plans.

What methods of production planning did you use?

If you have experience with formal planning methods such as PERT (Program Evaluation and Review Technique), use of Gannt charts, computer-based plans, describe them. If your planning experience is informal or of some specialized nature, discuss them and tell how they worked.

How were special or rush orders handled?

A good supervisor has to be able to roll with the punches. Flexibility is the key to success. Discuss how you were able to accomodate for special orders, how you met deadlines, made changes in the routine to satisfy customer's needs.

How close did you come to meeting your schedules last year? How do you account for your good (poor) performance? always on schedule? often? rarely?

If you have any figures to back up your response, show them. If you did not meet schedules, be prepared to defend your record. It is not necessary to become defensive or apologetic. Be frank about the situations that caused you to fall behind, and tell what you did to correct the situation and improve performance subsequently.

SUPERVISION

How large a group did you supervise? What job categories were included?

If you have had more than one position, be prepared to give these figures for each job you held. Indicate the number of people in each job category that you managed.

How did you maintain discipline in your department?

Describe your leadership style. Today, most companies prefer supervisors who are not martinets or bullies, nor do they want supervisors who are too easygoing. A middle-of-the-road approach is most acceptable. Be prepared to give examples of some of the disciplinary problems you had to handle.

How would you handle a situation where one of your workers changes from a reliable, hardworking employee to a problem person?

If you can illustrate this by giving an example of such a case, do so. If you have not had that experience, tell the interviewer this. As you might be asked to indicate what you might do if such a circumstance developed, think this one out before the interview. Remember the best answer would be to try to determine the cause and correct it so the employee would become productive again.

Your department has only white employees. A black worker is assigned to the department. You hear some grumbling among your old-timers. How will you handle this?

The purpose of such a question is to see if you indicate personal racial biases and also to test you in a delicate situation. Prepare yourself to respond with sensitivity and diplomacy.

How did you convey information to your employees?

Describe your communication approach. This could be purely a one-to-one oral communication, or it could be by group meetings, or through written instructions. Discuss each of the applicable approaches.

What responsibility did you have for training new employees? for ongoing training?

As training is an important supervisory function, tell what training you did yourself, what you did in conjunction with training specialists, etc. Be sure to include not only initial training of new employees but also continuing training of your people to keep them productive and to prepare them for advancement.

Factory Personnel (skilled workers)

MACHINISTS

What types of machines have you operated?

Specify all the machines on which you have experience.

What tolerances have you worked with?
What responsibility have you had for maintaining your machines?

Some operators can set up their machines, make minor adjustments, and repair breakdowns when they occur. Others only operate the machine and must call on a mechanic if servicing has to be done. Indeed, some union contracts prohibit operators from servicing machines. Be prepared to discuss all of your capabilities with machinery that you can.

How did you make out on an average in your incentive pay?

Many production jobs have incentive bonuses. If you have earned such bonuses, tell the interviewer how much, how often, and what was required to earn them.

Tell me about your background in shop math, blueprint reading.

If you used shop math and can read blueprints, tell about your education or experience in these areas.

What experience do you have in designing tools, dies, or machinery?

Highly skilled tool and die makers are in great demand. If you have any background in this work, even if it is not recent, be sure to let the employer know about it.

TOOL AND DIE MAKERS

What types of tools have you designed and made?

The tool and die maker is the elite of the machinist category. Workers with a heavy background in this field are invaluable. If this is your background, tell about the types of tools, dies, molds, and other equipment you created.

Tell me about the toughest problem you had and what you did to handle it.

If you have designed special tools to meet special purposes, tell what the problem was, how you approached it and how the tool you designed solved the problem.

TECHNICIANS

Technicians differ from other skilled workers in that they usually have had more formal schooling than apprentice training. Technicians are used in electronics plants, chemical plants, and other high-technology areas.

What courses have you completed in your field of work? Describe some of the projects you worked on.

As course names are sometimes misleading, describe each course briefly, tell where it was taken, and how long it lasted. Describe some of the projects on which you worked and, if pertinent, work-study projects in which you participated.

For what activities in your last job did you have full responsibility?

Describe the work you have done in each of the jobs you have had. Be specific. The employer will be impressed by your depth of knowledge about your field. Use technical language to show that you have the command of the lingo of the field.

With what equipment have you worked?

Mention all of the various types of equipment used. If you only have superficial knowledge of an important piece of equipment, tell the interviewer that. Do not claim experience where you do not have it, but indicate a willingness to learn new things. This impression can be reinforced by describing how you were able to absorb new information and technology rapidly in the past.

What plans do you have for taking additional study in your field?

Express your interest in getting as much additional training as you can to keep up with the state of the art in your field and to acquire additional skills and knowledge where they apply.

File Clerk

What types of filing systems have you used?

The interviewer will want to know if you have worked with alphabetic, numerical, subject files, or any special systems you are familiar with.

What departments did these files serve?

Did your filing system cover the entire company's work, or was it limited to just one department such as personnel, accounting, engineering?

How heavy was the volume of your files?

Did you work on the filing all day long? If not, how much time each day was devoted to filing? If your job had spurts of activity when you were very busy and times when things were light, tell the interviewer about how you handled the pressures of the heavy periods. If you have worked under time pressures in the past, it would be an asset if the job for which you are applying calls for this type of activity.

What sort of documents did you file?

Were they letters? legal documents? checks? invoices? complex reports?

How many file clerks were there in your department?

If your department was large, tell how the work was divided. If you handled specialized parts of the work or shared in all of it, and specify what your responsibilities were.

Did you work with a numerical or subject file? If so, did you participate in coding the material? What type of coding system was used?

If you are familiar with the Dewey Decimal System or

other formal systems, be sure to let the employer know about it. If there was a special system in your company, tell how it worked. If you did the coding or helped in it, be sure to bring this out.

What other duties did you perform?

Tell about all of your duties, including typing (even if you only typed labels for the files), receptionist or telephone relief, clerical duties other than filing, etc. In many jobs it is good to have diversified experience.

Marketing Manager

The functions of a marketing manager differ somewhat from industry to industry. The following questions are likely to be asked of candidates for this type of job in any consumer-oriented business.

Tell me about a successful marketing campaign which you conducted.

In describing this program be sure to tell the major problems you faced, how you approached them, and the results attained. Tell why you thought this campaign was particularly successful and how you measured its success. What share of the market did you obtain as a result of the program? Tell how it met other objectives, such as broadening your product line or expanding the market. Also be prepared to answer questions about unsuccessful campaigns and to discuss why they did not succeed.

What were your highest priorities in your last job? Why did you consider them important?

If your chief priority was to increase sales, tell what that would have meant to the company in terms of meeting its objectives. If your priorities were in other areas such as advertising and administration, tell why.

Describe the organizational setup of your department.

As a marketing manager, your managerial responsibilities are of concern to a prospective employer. Tell who reported to you and the structure of each subordinate level of management.

What was your specific responsibility for advertising?

Some marketing managers take a direct part in writing, placing, or editing copy; others just provide broad guidelines to subordinate specialists. Discuss your role in this function. If you worked closely with ad agencies, tell about how you did so. If you developed a particularly successful advertising program, tell about it and indicate your role. The more specific information you can give an interviewer, the better impression you will make.

Give some examples of new products you introduced or new markets in which you introduced your company's line.

New-product or new-market introductions are major challenges to marketing people. If you have this experience, it will show your creativity, initiative, and effectiveness in a critical area of the job.

What was your role in managing or supervising the sales force of your company?

Sales are an important part of the marketing function. Some marketing people are very strong in advertising and planning but weak in sales. However, if you are not a strong sales manager, discuss your experience in working with sales managers, guiding them to meet marketing objectives, and cooperating with them so that sales and other marketing functions are coordinated.

What types of sales promotion (other than media advertising) have you used?

Give examples (and show samples if possible) of direct mail promotions, point-of-purchase displays, trade show exhibits, etc.

What types of market research did your company do?

If your market research was done in-house, discuss the types of programs and your part in analyzing results. If it was contracted to outside firms, tell how you coordinated with them.

Mechanical Engineer

With what types of mechanical engineering are you most familiar?

As some M.E.'s have a wide variety of experiences, whereas others have become very specialized, this question is designed to obtain a good idea of your overall background. To make the most favorable impression, find out what the company is most interested in and emphasize the most closely related aspects of your background.

Tell me about some of the products you designed?

If these products or parts of products can be shown by samples, photographs, drawings, or blueprints, your presentation will be more impressive. However, if any of your work is confidential, tell the interviewer you cannot discuss it. Most employers will respect you for this decision.

What patents do you hold or what items did you develop on which your former company holds patents?

What experience have you had in recommending modifications on existing designs? in making these modifications?

Tell why you believed modifications were required, what you did, and what resulted. Give specific examples.

Describe your background in using computers in design and development work.

If you have this experience, tell how you either used the computer in your original design work or used it in testing the feasibility of the design before putting it into production.

What has been you experience in developing manufacturing processes?

Discuss how you attacked problems of this nature and give some examples.

What experience or background do you have in making environmental analyses?

Government regulations have made these analyses extremely important. Any exposure to this area should be brought out.

Tell me about your experience in handling safety programs.

Did you supervise such activities for your employer? Did you evaluate machines or equipment for safety defects? Any area of safety, from design and development to inspection and safety consciousness programs, should be mentioned.

What background do you have with working on projects that impose government specifications?

If you have worked with military specifications (mil-specs), ASME (American Society of Mechanical Engineers) specs, or other similar controls, bring it out with examples of problems you had in compliance and how you handled them.

What have you done in the area of writing instruction manuals for users of the equipment manufactured by your company?

Examples of instruction sheets, manuals, etc., should be brought to the interview to demonstrate your work.

What responsibility did you have for the supervision of other engineers? of drafting personnel? of others?

Show where you were on the organizational chart. Tell who reported to you and be prepared to answer questions about your supervisory and management techniques.

What part did you play in budgets? cost controls? other administrative (nonengineering) activities?

If such activity was a part of your job, tell what you contributed to the success of your department or organization in nontechnical aspects of the work.

Nurse

Tell me about your duties in your previous jobs.

This overview question will bring out what you have done and will serve as the basis for the rest of the interview questions. Before going for an interview, review your background and systematize your various experiences, so that you can talk about each of them in detail rather than floating from one to another and missing key points. If all your work was general hospital nursing, you can discuss the work you did in each of your jobs by comparing one to another (if you had more than one hospital assignment). If you specialized in a specific type of nursing, talk about your specialty.

What background do you have in . . . ?

Some of the areas you may be asked about include operating room assistance, intensive care units, emergency or traumatic care, pediatrics, geriatrics, obstetrics, and anesthesiology. In answering this question, be prepared to give examples of some of the cases you worked on that point out your strengths in that type of work.

Other than hospital work, what type of nursing experience have you had?

If you worked as an industrial nurse, private-care nurse, visiting nurse, psychiatric nurse, etc., at any time in your career, tell about it.

Tell me about your post-graduate training in your field.

Include in-service courses, seminars and workshops, courses taken in colleges or special institutes, and any other specialized training in medical technology, equipment, nursing techniques, etc.

What responsibility did you have in supervising the work of others?

If you were a charge nurse and supervised other R.N.'s or your regular duties included supervising the work of nurses' aides or medical technicians, tell about it. Even if you did not have a supervisory title, if your work required directing the work of other people, tell the interviewer about it.

What experience have you had in keeping records of narcotics dispensing and use?

Describe the procedures with which you are familiar in this area.

How did you assist physicians in physical examinations? treatment? preparing patients for various medical procedures?

Tell about your role in these activities. Give examples of unusual cases which illustrate your expertise.

What background do you have in handling medicare and insurance claims and paperwork?

With more and more of nurses' time taken with administrative matters, knowledge of these areas is an asset.

What aspect of nursing most appeals to you? appeals least to you?

These twin questions are designed to determine if the duties of the open position are in line with your likes or dislikes. If you can determine in advance of the interview the nature of the job, you can tailor your response accordingly or withdraw from the job if it requires you to spend much of your time in areas not to your liking.

In addition to the preceding questions, be prepared to answer technical questions on various aspects of nursing technology.

Office Manager

Office managers are likely to be asked questions about their responsibilities for supervising others and their control of the work of their departments.

What types of positions were under your jurisdiction?

Don't just answer with vague information such as, "I supervised clerks and typists." Be specific about the duties of your staff.

How many people have you supervised?

If the job calls for supervising many people and you have only supervised a few, try to convince the employer that techniques of supervision are similar no matter how many people are in a department.

What criteria did you use in selecting personnel for your staff?

If you had firm job specifications, discuss them; tell how they were developed and how you measured the background of applicants against these specifications.

Describe your method of motivating people.

Are you an autocratic or a permissive leader or somewhere in between. The best way to discuss this is to give examples of situations in which your method of motivation worked well.

What method did you use in appraising employees?

If your former (or present) company has a formal appraisal program, discuss it and tell how you used it in your own appraisals of employees. If it was an informal system or one you developed yourself, describe it in detail.

Give me an example of some of the problems you had in supervising your staff.

Select problems that you approached creatively and solved. You may be asked to tell about some of the tough ones you could not solve. As most jobs have such situations, don't avoid telling about failures, but emphasize that they were only an insignificant segment of the total picture.

What responsibility did you have in orienting and training new people?

Was training done on the job or in special programs? What part did you play in this training? If you developed programs, methods, or other training activities, discuss them. Let the interviewer know about your use of training aids such as audiovisual equipment, closed-circuit TV, case studies, and seminars. If you wrote or helped write training materials or manuals, bring along copies to show the prospective employer.

Discuss your staff's record of turnover. To what do you attribute this (good or poor) record?

Be able to explain the reasons people left your company (or department). Even if the company had a high rate of turnover, if your department's record was significantly better than other departments' records, it will make you look good.

How did you establish work schedules?

If your work was routine, tell how you kept it going along smoothly. If it was the kind of work load that varied, tell how you handled special situations that resulted.

Tell me about the systems and procedures you developed. How did they improve the work flow?

Any improvements you made in processing paper, eliminating work, or reducing cost or time for jobs under your jurisdiction should be discussed with as many specific examples as possible.

What other assignments did you have? Did you have them regularly? only on occasion?

Many officer managers are given special projects. If you have had to make surveys, develop a new program, or help other department heads with their problems, this experience will give you added ammunition in selling yourself to the employer.

What exposure have you had to EDP?

Because of the growing importance of data processing to all business operations, any background in any aspect of data processing should be emphasized. This includes working with any type of terminal, using or supervising the use of word-processing machines, or interfacing with computer personnel.

What responsibility did you have for purchasing? for what items?

Most office managers purchase office supplies and equipment. If you have done this or have worked closely with your firm's purchasing staff in such purchases, tell what equipment, how you made decisions on what to purchase, how much money you could spend without approval from above, and other relevant matters.

What types of office equipment have been under your jurisdiction?

Discuss any equipment with which your people worked, even if you are not an expert in operating the machine yourself.

Personnel Manager

Questions for personnel managers or assistants usually are divided among the functions of the job.

EMPLOYMENT

Describe your company's policies on internal sources of recruitment. What did you do in this program?

Tell about your experience with job posting, skill banks, employee referrals, etc.

What levels of job categories did you seek to fill?

Indicate if they were primarily clerical, technical, managerial, etc. Also note what salary parameters were involved.

What sources did you use?

Discuss your experience in working with employment agencies, executive recruiters, unions, etc. If you wrote want ads, tell what type of ads (bring samples if you have any of which you are particularly proud), where they were placed, and what results were attained. If you have college recruiting, minority recruiting, or other special experience, be sure to bring it out.

Secretaries are in short supply. One of our executives is pressing the personnel department to find him a secretary. What steps would you take to find him one?

This is a situational question. A good response: "I'd study the job specifications to assure that they are realistic. If not, I'd discuss the job with the executive to find out just what he/she really needs. I'd examine any ads used to see if they could be improved. If employment agencies have been contacted, I'd check to find out what they are doing to fill the job. I'd determine if any sources have been neglected and then get to work to utilize all possible means of recruiting the type of person desired." (see chapter 5 for further explanation).

WAGE AND SALARY

Tell me about the compensation system in your present (or previous) company.

If it was a formal system, be prepared to discuss it. If informal, tell how it was established and used.

What responsibility did you have for the compensation system?

If you were the one to introduce and develop the system, tell how you went about doing it. If your main responsibility was the implementation of an established system, describe some of the problems you had and how you handled them. Also tell about changes you made (if any) and the reasons for them.

For what types of jobs have you written job descriptions?

If you have some examples to bring along, do so.

What formal job evaluation systems have you used? Describe them. With what other systems are you familiar?

Point systems, factor comparison systems, and variations on these are the ones most frequently used, so if you have background in any of these, be prepared to discuss them. If your company had an informal system, discuss it and try to show how close it may be to a better-known program.

EMPLOYEE RELATIONS (NONUNION)

How did you cope with turnover? absenteeism? lateness?

Give examples and, where possible, statistics that show how your company kept these problems to a minimum.

What was your responsibility for employee communications?

If you edited or contributed to the house organ, bring copies and show just what you did. Booklets, letters, bulletins, or other forms of communication should be handled the same way. If pertinent, tell about your experience in employee attitude surveys, suggestions systems, etc.

Morale in our packing department is very low. What steps would you take to correct it?

Another situational question. Good response: "I'd find the informal leaders in the department and win their confidence. You can obtain a great deal of real information from such people which will help identify problems so that proper solutions can be developed." (see chapter 5 for explanation).

LABOR RELATIONS

What experience have you had in dealing with labor unions? At what level of the union hierarchy did you deal?
At what point did you become involved informally? in a formal grievance? What was your role in arbitration?

All of these questions are geared to determine your role in the day-to-day relations with the union. Name the union(s) with which you have worked. Tell about special problems and emphasize how you succeeded in resolving grievances.

What part did you play in contract negotiations?

Contract negotiations require special skills and experience. Many organizations have specialists to do this work. If you have any background in this area, give details, including specific examples of contracts in which you either participated as a negotiator or were the principal spokesperson for you company.

MISCELLANEOUS

Safety: What responsibility have you had for safety programs? for OSHA (Occupational Safety and Health Administration) compliance?

Safety has become a specialized field and in many companies personnel people have nothing to do with it. If you have experience, discuss it. But if safety came under your authority only as an administrative function, tell who actually did the safety work and just what part you played in its administration.

Equal employment: Describe your company's affirmative action program. What was your part in it?

EEO (equal employment opportunity) and affirmative action are a key part of every personnel position today. They are not the same, so they must be explained separately. If your company had an affirmative action program, discuss how it was established (if you were involved), how you worked to implement it, the problems faced and how they were handled, etc. If there was no affirmative action program, tell how you kept your company aware of EEO policies.

Have you compiled EEO-1 reports? What experience have you had in handling complaints from state or federal EEO officials?

Discuss your resonsibility for keeping these records. Tell about any cases brought against you and how you resolved them.

Unemployment insurance-workers' compensation: What responsibility did you have for unemployment insurance claims? workers' compensation claims? Have you appeared at hearings for these claims?

Be prepared to discuss your experience in these areas with as much detail as needed to show your expertise.

Exit interviews: What information did you seek at an exit interview? How did you apply what you learned to personnel policy?

Specific examples of information gleaned from exit interviews that helped shape personnel policy should be given.

Testing: With what selection tests are you familiar? How do you feel about tests as a selection service?

Be prepared to discuss the validity of these tests and the ways you measured their effectiveness.

Personnel records: For what personnel records were you responsible? Have you any background with computerized personnel files? What forms did you develop or change in you previous positions?

Orientation: Describe what your company did to orient new employees to the company. What role did you play in this activity?

If you conducted orientation programs, tell what you did. If you wrote orientation manuals, bring samples. If you used films, tapes, etc., tell about them.

Training: For what training programs did you have responsibility? Describe your specific role in these programs.

Did you develop the programs? Conduct the programs? Arrange for outside presentations? Describe these programs and tell about their effectiveness.

What management development techniques have you used? With what others are you familiar?

Talk about those techniques with which you are familiar, such as MBO, Management Grid, simulations, or case studies.

Plant Manager

What type of facility did you manage?

As the job of plant manager differs from plant to plant depending upon the size of the plant, process of manufacturing, and products produced, questions will focus on these areas before going into depths of personal responsibilities. Describe your facility. Was it a process operation like a chemical or paper mill? An assembly operation like an automobile plant or a job order facility that manufactures products on special orders? Be prepared to describe the manufacturing process and talk about the products manufactured.

What was the size of your plant?

Give the number of plants over which you had control, the number of employees in each facility, the physical size of the plant(s), the number of intermediate managers and their positions.

What type of operations did you manage?

Discuss the various operations such as stamping, welding, cut-and-sew, painting, finishing, assembling, and packaging.

What was your responsibility for production planning? Tell me about your experience in plant layout. What responsibility did you have for specifying machinery or equipment to be purchased? for purchasing same?

These questions cover certain aspects of plant management that are sometimes handled by others than the plant manager. If you did these yourself, give details; if you managed others who were responsible for each or any of these areas, tell just what part you played in managing the specialists involved.

What systems and procedures did you establish to cut costs? How did you introduce them? How did they work?

The answer to this question can show your creativity. Tell what the previous system was, what you did to change it and resolve any problems, and the results attained.

What unions represented your employees? What part did you play in negotiating the contracts? What part did you play in day-to-day relations with the union? Tell me about some of the more difficult problems you had in your union relations.

When there is a union contract, the plant manager is the chief line executive who deals with the union. Support is available from personnel or industrial relations specialists, but the plant manager has final responsibility at a particular plant. Discuss your experience in all phases of union-management relations, emphasizing those areas where you won important gains for your company.

What types of gripes and grievances did your people bring to you? How did you handle them? Did unions attempt to organize your people?

When there is no union, the management has an even more difficult job solving morale problems and settling gripes and grievances to prevent the employees from being organized by a union. Discuss some of the things you did to keep your people satisfied, to keep gripes from becoming grievances, and, if pertinent, specific things you did to combat union-organizing drives.

Describe the organizational setup in your company. Tell me about your approach to directing your people.

What special problems did you have with your supervisors or staff managers? How did you handle them?

All managers must get things done through other people. Higher-level managers must get things accomplished by using the best talents of their subordinate managers. Tell about your approach to getting results through others. Specific examples will make the answer to this question more meaningful to the interviewer.

Programmers
TRAINEES

What schooling have you had in programming?

Tell whether it was at college level or in a specialized training school. Tell about what the courses entailed, what types of equipment were used, what languages were studied, etc. If your training was on the job or in the military service, discuss how the training was conducted and what you learned.

What equipment did your school have?

If you have not given this information in your response to the first question, detail the types of equipment by manufacturer and model. Include both mainframe and peripheral equipment that you know.

What languages have you studied?

As computer languages are the basic tool of the programmer, tell not only what languages you have studied but also how well you know them. If the language used on the job for which you are applying is different from your training, emphasize that you learn rapidly and could readily pick up the needed language. Many companies expect to train "trainee programmers" in their language, but prefer persons who have some background in BASIC or another of the languages taught in the schools.

Describe your experience in work-study programs, in school projects.

Students who have had the opportunity to engage in work-study programs with companies have the advantage of gaining practical experience while still in school. If you are fortunate enough to have had this training, be sure to tell as much as possible about just what you did on that assignment. This experience is tantamount to having had a position in the field and gives you a competitive edge over other trainees. If you did not participate in a work-study program, but did work on a significant programming project in school, discuss it in detail. Often it gives students worthwhile background that is almost equivalent to a job.

What courses have you had in math? Accounting? Science?

Many applicants for trainee programmer positions do not have any formal training in programming in school. Courses in math, science, and accounting are looked upon by employers as good background for developing the skills needed in programming. If you did well in these courses, it should be emphasized.

What were your hobbies, extracurricular activities, etc.?

Hobbies such as chess, playing bridge, solving puzzles, and similar interests are looked upon as predictors of potential in programming.

EXPERIENCED PROGRAMMERS

What equipment have you used?

If the equipment on which you are experienced is different from that used by the company to which you are applying, try to sell the employer on the transferability of your skills. It is a good idea to learn about equipment other than your own, so that you can talk intelligently about how your knowledge can be used effectively even with equipment different from the ones on which you worked.

What languages have you used? studied?

Indicate the languages you used on previous jobs as well as others with which you have familiarity. Emphasize the skill you have in each language.

What were the applications of your programs?

Is your experience primarily commercial? Technical? Scientific? If commercial, tell about the specific utilization (e.g., payroll, inventory control, forecasting). If technical, discuss how it was used in product design, testing reliability, etc. If scientific, discuss its nature.

Did you supervise, train, or direct other programmers?

If you have supervisory or management experience, tell how many people were supervised, how you managed them, what responsibility you had in scheduling and checking the work of others, etc.

On what sort of data base did you work?

Discuss the size and nature of the data base.

Tell me about your background or experience in other phases of data processing.

Here is your chance to tell about those special phases of EDP in which you have experience or knowledge. Talk about background with MIS (Management Information System), DOS (Disk Operating System), real time, time-sharing, software design, and any other education, experience, or knowledge that makes you stand out.

Public Relations
TRAINEES

What special educational background do you have related to public relations?

Courses in public relations, writing, journalism, and similar subjects are obviously good background. Also, courses requiring written reports in areas close to the company's field of interest are helpful. These might include economics, business administration, science, market research, etc.

Other than required papers, what writing have you done?

Discuss what kinds of things you have written for school papers or magazines. What editorial responsibility have you had? A big plus would be published works in nonscholastic publications.

Describe what you consider your most creative accomplishments so far in your life.

Think carefully about this before the interview. Be prepared to discuss what you have done, which you believe will illustrate your creativity. If it was an idea or concept, discuss how it was implemented. If it was a written work, what was done to get it published? If the idea had to be sold to somebody else, tell what you did to sell it.

What responsibility have you had for setting up programs?

Describe meetings, press conferences, and special functions that you arranged.

EXPERIENCED PR PEOPLE

What sort of speeches have you written?

If this was part of your job, tell the type of speech (technical, political, general), for whom the speeches were written, and if you gave them yourself. In all cases, identify the audience for which it was written, whether it received press or TV coverage, and other pertinent data.

Describe your community relations programs.

Community relations is often an important component of the PR manager's job. Tell about the community projects in which you were involved, what public officials you worked with, the purpose of the project, and how effective it was.

What responsibility did you have for stockholders' meetings?

If you set up stockholders' meetings, tell what you did. If you were involved with stockholder problems or part of a proxy battle, be sure to talk about it.

With what news media do you have good relationships?

Contacts with the media in your area can be a major asset in getting the job. Talk about how you used the media, what special favors you did for editors or TV producers, and what they have done for you. Don't use this as a name-dropping exercise. You should have good connections with the people mentioned.

What were some of the unusual projects you developed? How did you sell them to management? With what results?

Here is your chance to show your creative side from a practical viewpoint. Some of the types of projects you might have developed would be tie-ins with national or regional events (e.g., bi-centennial programs, the Winter Olympics, local sporting events). Other notable PR projects could be press coverage of surveys made by your company and articles about special activities your company sponsored.

In your opinion, what were your most important contributions to the corporate image your company wanted to project?

If this question is not asked, find an opportunity to tell the interviewer what you think was your most important contribution and why it was significant.

Receptionist-Telephone Operator

Receptionists usually do more than just sit at a desk and greet visitors to the company. They may have to perform a variety of clerical tasks, take messages for people who are not in the office, type documents, and in many cases, operate the telephone switchboard.

Tell me about the types of situations you faced on a typical day.

Be prepared to tell about both usual situations and unusual problems that you handled. Some examples: "When customers came with complaints or inquiries, I made sure they were courteously treated and were directed to the person in the office who could help them," or "I diplomatically got rid of solicitors, peddlers, and others who might disturb our people."

What kinds of people did you greet?

Were they salespersons? applicants for employment? others?

What other duties did you perform?

Describe all of the clerical duties, special projects, etc., that you worked on.

A pesty salesperson comes in several times a week at the regular time the purchasing agent has allotted for seeing vendors. The purchasing agent does not want to see this solicitor. How would you handle it?

This is a situational question. Some responses: "Thank you for coming by, however our company does not use the product you sell, so it would not be to your advantage to wait to see our purchasing agent." or "Mr. Malone is familiar with your product. He will be happy to contact you if he needs more information." (see chapter 5 for explanation).

What is your typing speed?

Can you use a dictating machine?

How many persons did you greet on a typical day?

If the person the caller wanted to see or speak to was not in, what did you do?

Tell if you referred the caller to someone else, made an appointment for a future time, or took a message.

What types of switchboards have you used?

Indicate the specific name or number of the boards with which you have had experience. Describe any unusual equipment you used.

How many positions did the board have?

Indicate if you were the only operator or if there were others working at the same time.

How many trunks and extensions did your board have?

To what degree did you handle overseas calls?

What other responsibilities did you have as a receptionist?

Describe clerical, receptionist, or other duties.

What other equipment have you worked with?

Knowledge of teletype, facsimile, EDP hookups, etc., is an asset.

What responsibility did you have for checking phone bills?

If you have saved your company money by checking bills or settling problems with the phone company, give details about it.

In your company, how were the long-distance calls handled?

Did you place all the calls or just those with special problems? If you kept records of long-distance calls, describe how these records were kept.

How busy was your board?

Was it a slow, steady activity or a hectic and sporadic pace?

Retail Salesperson

What products did you sell?

What hours and days did you work?

What was your responsibility for setting up point-of-purchase advertising material? preparing merchandise for display on the shelves or counters?

If you have experience in these areas, describe them in detail.

What were the average daily receipts at your counter or department? Was customer flow steady or irregular?

Try to find out before the interview what type of customer flow the store with the job opening has. In the interview, play up your experience in dealing with the type of customer flow required by the employer.

What responsibility did you have for approving credit sales? Did your store have its own credit facilities or did it use bank or credit card services (e.g., Visa, Mastercard)?

How much money could you approve on your own? If all credit decisions were made by a credit department, say so.

With what types of cash registers are you familiar?

Use proper manufacturers name and model numbers.

How did you handle customer complaints? Give me an example of a problem you may have had with an irate customer and how you handled it.

Dealing with customers is the key responsibility of a salesperson. Be prepared to give some examples of how you saved a customer for the store or in other ways maintained good customer relations.

What was the toughest sale you made in the last six months? What was the problem and how did you solve it?

Before going on an interview, review your experience and be prepared to tell about tough sales, how you turned a customer around, or how you salvaged an almost-lost sale.

How much of your earnings were from salary? from incentive? How did you compare with other persons in your department?

The success of persons working on commission or incentives is measured by their earnings. Expect to be asked to divulge this information.

What prizes, contests, premiums from manufacturers, etc., did you win?

Such prizes are symbols of success. Don't be modest. Talk about them proudly, but not in a bragging manner.

How did you develop new customers? maintain contact with CU's? What responsibility did you have for advertising and sales promotion? merchandising? store management?

If you have used direct mail, personal letters, telephone contact with regular customers, describe how you used them. Bring samples of letters if pertinent. If you had managerial or merchandising responsibilities, be sure the employer is told about them.

What aspect of your job was most challenging for you? Why? What aspect of your work did you find most unsatisfactory? Why?

Think about these questions carefully before going on an interview. Make sure your answer indicates that you are challenged by things this new job will offer and that you don't find unsatisfactory the phases of the work that are most needed. (If the latter is the case, it is better to withdraw.) Salespersons who have sold high-ticket items or specialized merchandise such as furs, jewelry, furniture, audio components, and appliances should also be prepared to answer questions on technical or special knowledge about these items.

Retail Store Manager
MERCHANDISING

What product lines were you responsible for merchandising?

If you were a specialist in one or a few lines, tell about them and be specific as to the nature of the lines. If you have a more general background, let the interviewer know the variety of merchandise you handled.

What experience have you had in utilizing (or creating) displays and other point-of-purchase materials?

If possible, bring pictures of some of these items with you to the interview.

Tell me about (show me) some of the ads you wrote for your store.

Any statistics you can provide showing the effectiveness of the ad will strengthen your position.

BUYING

What responsibility did you have for ordering new merchandise (as against replacing sold items)? On what basis did you make these decisions? What sources did you use? Up to how much money could you spend without approval from higher management?

Describe your buying systems, innovations you made in types of merchandise carried, how you developed new and unusual sources, etc.

MARKETING

What was the sales volume of your store? How did it compare with others in the chain? To what do you

*attribute this difference? What responsibility did you
have for marking down merchandise? for running ads
for merchandise? for determining when a sale should
be held?*

In preparing for the interview, review your record.
Bring with you or prepare to discuss your track record
and what you did to make this record as good as it was, or
to defend it if it was unsatisfactory.

SUPERVISION AND TRAINING

*How many salespeople were in your store? How
many other personnel? Tell me about some of the
problems you had in hiring, retaining, and managing
your people.*

Emphasize how you solved the tough personnel
problems, how you kept your store staffed, etc.

*What responsibility did you have in recruiting and
selecting your staff? What criteria did you use in
making a hiring decision?*

If the personnel department did most of the screening,
tell on what basis you made the final hiring decisions.

*How did you train your new people? What types of
continuing training programs did your company have?
What part did you play in this training?*

Employers are more concerned with training in sales
techniques, customer relations, and personal development on the job than with routine training (e.g., filling
out sales slips, operating cash registers).

*What types of specific problems did you have in
directing your people?*

Tell about your management style. How did you get people to do their jobs most effectively? What problems did you solve that made your people more productive? Kept down turnover?

INVENTORY AND COST CONTROL

Describe your inventory control system. What part did you play in keeping the inventory of your store? What was the turnover of various items?

What were the various cost factors in your store (rent, utilities, advertising, payroll, etc.)? What was the ratio of costs of gross volume? During your tenure as manager, how did this change?

If you had no store operations responsibility, say so. If the figures were confidential, explain this to the interviewer. Most employers will respect you for maintaining confidences.

The following questions may be asked to persons with specific background in the fields mentioned. As always, be as specific as possible and bring examples where applicable.

Apparel: What responsibility did you have for fashion shows? Were they run in the store or off the premises? Tell me about them. What other special promotions did you use to promote your lines?

Hard goods: What manufacturers did your store represent? What types of cooperative advertising did you use? Tell me about some of the major promotions you ran?

Mass merchandising stores (food, variety, etc.): How did you determine which items should receive more or better shelf space? Tell me about your problems in promoting housebrands or other nonnationally advertised merchandise.

Department or chain stores: Describe your system of interstore coordination. What experience have you had with computer-based systems?

Salesperson

What products have you sold?

Be prepared to answer questions testing your knowledge of these products.

What markets have you called on?

If you have called on industrial companies, you may be asked questions about the persons in those companies with whom you dealt, such as purchasing agents, plant managers, and engineers. If you have called on stores to sell products for resale, be prepared to talk about how you helped the retailers merchandise your products. Give specific examples wherever possible.

What customers have you called on?

Naming specific customers gives the employer a good idea of the nature of your experience. If your customers were all one type of company and the interviewing company sells to similar customers, it will be an asset. Try to find out the kind of customers served by a prospective employer before the interview and emphasize aspects of your background that would enable you to sell to those markets. Naming customers also helps the interviewer relate better to what you have done, particularly when they are in the same or similar businesses as customers of your prospective employer.

Where did you get your leads?

Some companies provide leads to salespersons; in others, each salesperson must dig up the leads. Describe how you developed business.

What was the volume in your territory when you took it over? when you left?

If it had increased, tell how you did it; if it decreased, be prepared to explain why.

How did you do in relation to other salespeople in your company?

Tell about contests or competitions you won, about bonuses or extra compensation earned and, if you know, the way you rated against your peers.

Tell me about the toughest sale you ever made.

Tell what made it so tough and how you closed the sale.

What was the most unexpected objection you ever got from a prospect and how did you handle it?

Questions like this are geared to take you by surprise and see your reaction. It also shows the employer your ability to handle the unexpected on the job. In preparing for an interview, think of special cases which may be referred to when asked this type of question.

If you were training a new person to take over your territory, what facts about your customers would you stress?

This gives the employer insight into your knowledge of your customers. Tell about each customer's strengths and weaknesses and their personal idiosyncrasies.

A major long-term customer tells you that a competitor offered him a substantial kickback. It has been a firm policy of your company not to give kickbacks. How would you handle it?

This issue is very sensitive. It is always safe to be conservative and cautious in answering this type of question.

Your competitor starts a major ad campaign. Your ad support is minimal. How can you combat this?

If you have faced this problem in the past, tell what

you did. If not, talk about more effective selling, better customer relations, etc.

Your biggest customer moves out of your territory. How would you go about replacing this business?

Talk about sales development and prospecting approaches.

How do you feel about out-of-town travel?

If it is necessary for the job and you do not like to travel, withdraw from consideration.

What is your family's attitude about your being away several days (weeks) at a time?

Unless your family will back you up, a job of this sort is not for you.

How do you feel about air travel? driving long hours?

Again, be sure the travel requirements of the job are in line with your objectives.

How do you feel about working on a compensation plan that is chiefly commission?

If you have worked on commission before, discuss how it worked for you. If not, be sure you understand what the probable earnings will be for both the short and the long term.

What is it you particularly like about selling? dislike about selling?

Think carefully before answering this question. You may like the fact that you are outside and not under a boss' constant surveillance, but it is not good to say so because it may be interpreted in a different way than you meant. Good answers to the first part of the question could be the challenge of making a sale, the compensation, the ability to be creative. To the second part, select carefully the areas you dislike. Make sure they are not critical to the new job.

Secretary

Tell me how you spent a typical day on your job.

The answer to this question should give the interviewer an overview of your experience. Be thorough in your answer without getting too wordy. A succinct outline of the nature of your work in each of the jobs you have held should be prepared before you come to the interview, so you can answer this question easily and fluently.

How much of your work involved dictation and transcription?

Tell whether this was the major part of your work or a less important part, and whether it was by stenography or by dictating equipment.

What types of personal matters did you handle for your boss?

Some secretaries handle highly confidential matters, including personal correspondence and finances.

In what areas did you write your own correspondence?

Many executives prefer to let a secretary write the routine letters without their being dictated. If you have done correspondence this way, describe on what matters you wrote letters, the type of letters, and the extent of this activity.

What reports did you compile? In what way did you contribute to these reports?

Tell about reports you researched, those for which you compiled information, and those you actually wrote or typed. If you have experience in charts or statistical typing, mention it.

What special assignments did your boss give you?
How did you handle them?

A description of your special assignments will give the interviewer an opportunity to evaluate that part of your background, making you stand out from other competitors for the job. Be prepared to discuss these in detail.

In what ways did you contribute to your boss'
(department's) success?

Answers to this could include such things as, "I made sure no deadlines were missed," or "I helped prepare materials for presentation to higher management." Give details.

Tell me about some of the problems you encountered on your last job or on previous jobs.

Include problems of dealing with your boss' subordinates or superiors, problems with customers or vendors, or any other problems you *successfully* handled.

Secretary to a sales manager: Discuss your responsibilities regarding customer inquiries or complaints. How did you deal with salespeople's problems?

Specific information on those aspects of your job that were related to the sales department's activities should be related.

Secretary to a purchasing manager: Tell me how you handled salespeople who wanted to see your boss.

Often this requires diplomacy and tact. Tell how you kept your busy boss on schedule. Discuss any details of the purchasing activity that your performed, including record keeping, actual buying, inventory control, etc.

Secretary to a controller: What accounting records did you keep?

Discuss the financial records you kept, the accounting equipment with which you are familiar, and responsibilities you had in this work other than just secretarial.

Secretary to a staff of senior executives: Have you taken transcripts of meetings? Have you taken minutes of meetings?

Discuss what sort of meetings, how detailed your notes were, who they were presented to, and the pressures involved.

Secretary to corporate counsel: Have you prepared legal briefs? court proceedings? What has your experience been in preparing contracts? leases? Tell me about the types of legal documents with which you are familiar.

Legal departments of companies require some knowledge of judicial procedures and legal language. If you have such experience, be sure to let the interviewer know about it.

Social Worker

What aspects of your education in social work have you found most important in your career?

Discuss both undergraduate and graduate studies that have been helpful to you. Give examples of how you applied your studies to specific cases.

What type of cases do you work with most frequently?

If you are a specialist in family problems, criminal rehabilitation, or problems of special concern to racial, ethnic, or religious groups or other specific phases of social work, discuss it in detail. If your work is of a general nature, pick out some of the more common areas of work and discuss them, but be sure to indicate your familiarity with other areas as well.

What sort of a case load do you usually carry?

Tell about your typical case load and also unusual situations which caused you to carry more (or less) at times.

What background have you had in family counseling?

Tell about your education and experience in this type of work. Also be prepared to give examples of some of your cases.

What background do you have in psychiatric social work?

If you do some of this (or are expert in it), give the interviewer an insight into your training and experience.

Tell me about the type of agency with which you are now (or have been) affiliated.

Was it a government or quasi-governmental agency? A religious-affiliated agency? A school- or university-based unit?

What experience do you have in administration of social work activities?

Describe your background in the paperwork functions and other areas such as budgeting, reporting to trustees, and office management.

Tell me about some of the cases which have given you difficulty and how you handled them.

Be prepared for such questions, and prior to going to an interview, review your cases so that you can select some that will give a good picture of your successes.

What experience have you had in . . .

These areas will cover every aspect of social work, including crisis intervention, parole work, diagnostic assessments, consultations with psychiatrists and other medical personnel, family counseling, family court assignments, welfare cases, pediatric cases, geriatric cases, etc. Review your education and experience and outline your background in each of the areas where you have worked. Review them again before each interview, so that you will be prepared to give detailed and satisfactory responses to these questions.

What experience have you had in training new counselors?

Discuss any formal or informal training you have given others, including subordinates, student interns, and even peers.

What background have you had in working with volunteers?

Tell what types of volunteers, what work you assigned them, what control you had over them, etc.

*Other than your counseling or social work activities,
what other services did you perform for your agency?*

Include here public relations, fund raising, community
or political coordination, etc.

Why did you choose to make a career in social work?

As a person in a helping profession, tell how your
desire to be a helping person has been satisfied in this
field, despite its frustrations.

Systems Analyst

Because most systems analysts have a background in programming, it is likely that you may be asked the same questions asked of programmers as well as those specific to the analysts job. Review the section on Programmers in this chapter and then prepare to answer questions like the following:

Give me some examples of specific systems you designed. For what applications were they used? How did you test your systems? On what sort of data bases have you worked? What experience have you had in feasibility studies? Describe your background in systems utilization. How did you decide what systems to develop?

Be prepared to answer the above questions with as specific information as you can. Each of these questions is designed to determine the depth of you experience. If you were part of a systems team, tell what the team did and then indicate your personal function.

What responsibility did you have for these programs after you designed them?

Tell about projects you initiated. If the problem was presented by the department head, tell when you became involved and just what you did.

Many people involved in specific operations resent and resist change. How did you overcome resistance to systems that you introduced?

This questions is designed to determine your human relations skills. In preparing for the interview, think about some of the personality problems you had to overcome with department heads and others and have some good examples ready to illustrate this phase of your background.

Describe your work in operations research.

Systems analysts with OR experience should tell about some of the models they constructed and how predictive they were.

What experience have you had in evaluating or purchasing software from outside sources?

Many companies purchase software from outside sources. This type of experience is important. If you have done this, tell from whom you purchased the software, on what basis you made the decision, and other relevant facts.

What experience have you had in analyzing and modifying programs currently in use by your company? Give some examples.

Why was the original program ineffective? How did you analyze it? What was your solution?

After developing systems, what part did you play in writing manuals or procedural instructions?

If possible, bring examples of manuals or instructions you have written.

What was your responsibility in following up on the progress of systems you developed?

Discuss the methods you had for follow-up. Give examples of how this resulted in redesign or modification.

Tell me about some of the conversions you participated in from manual systems to computer, from one type of computer to another.

As many companies are still in the process of converting from manual to computer systems, such a background could be important and useful.

Teacher

Teachers should expect questions related to their specialties (e.g., art, music, social sciences, physical sciences, languages), as well as pedagogical methods. The following are some general questions all teachers might be asked:

What areas of fundamental skills should a child have when completing sixth (or eighth or twelfth) grade?

This question could be answered generally to include basic reading, writing, and arithmetic skills or specifically to discuss your specialty.

How do you see your special field of teaching in relation to the entire educational process?

If you are a primary school teacher, you can talk about laying the groundwork for future education. If you are a teacher of a particular subject—such as art or science— you should show the relationship of that field to the total learning process.

Describe how you prepared your lessons.

If you worked from a detailed lesson plan, tell how you prepared and used it. If you used a system of modules, discuss how it worked. Any other approaches you had to making a lesson more exciting and meaningful should be brought out. Give examples where pertinent.

How would you individualize the needs of pupils with special problems?

Give examples of your approach.

Give some examples of how you utilized the special facilities of your school in your work.

Tell about your use of the library, audiovisual facilities, teaching specialists.

*How would you conduct a conference to report
student progress?*

Discuss how you worked with parents on their children's activities.

How did you handle behavior problems in your class?

With behavior problems becoming more and more of
a problem in many schools, think carefully about how
you effectively kept your class in order. Give good
examples both of cases where you prevented problems
and of those where the problems were not easily handled,
but you were successful in solving them.

*Tell me about some of the extracurricular activities
you supervised.*

If you coached a team, acted as advisor to a club or
other activity, bring it out. Any special commendations
or awards earned by your team or club or by you directly
should be mentioned.

*How do you view the role of the teacher in the school
of the future?*

This type of question is designed to determine your
philosophy of education, your optimism or pessimism,
and your concepts of adjusting to change. To prepare
yourself for such a queston, give some thought to your
feelings about how new technologies, different attitudes, and changes in the demographic makeup of your
community may affect education.

As teachers in each specialty area will be asked
different questions, your attention is called to the
following books used by school administrators to help
them determine what questions to ask applicants for
teaching jobs:

Interviewing and Selecting Elementary School Teachers and Administrative Personnel by Irwin Sadetsky and Arthur R. Pell

Interviewing and Selecting High School Teachers and Administrative Personnel by Thomas F. Rooney, Jr., and Arthur R. Pell

Interviewing and Selecting College and University Teachers and Administrative Personnel by L. Vernon Caine and Arthur R. Pell

All are published by Personnel Publications, P.O. Box 301, Huntington, N.Y. 11743.

CHAPTER 7

QUESTIONS FOR PEOPLE WITH LITTLE WORK EXPERIENCE

If you have no work experience or just one or two short-term jobs, the interview will have to focus on schooling, interests, personality, hobbies, extracurricular activities, and volunteer work. This subject will be broken down into the special problems of recent high school graduates, college graduates, and women entering or reentering the work force after raising a family.

HIGH SCHOOL GRADUATES

Most questions will center about your high school record. Be prepared to answer questions about grades, courses taken, teams or clubs to which you belonged, leadership roles, and part-time or summer jobs.

How were your grades in high school? Be truthful. Many firms will ask for copies of your report cards or will write to the schools for them. If you did not have good grades, don't give up and assume you are doomed to remain unemployed forever. You can handle poor grades in a variety of ways, depending upon the type of job for which you are applying. If the job is mechanical in nature, you might reply, "I have always been very good with mechanical things. My grades in shop courses were excellent, but I did have trouble with courses such as English and history because I just couldn't get interested in them." If your grades improved with the years, point it out: "You will notice that I did much better in the twelfth grade than the earlier grades. I wasn't too interested in school at first, but as I got older, I really began to take an interest and it showed up in my grades."

In what subjects did you do best? do least well? Be prepared to discuss why you performed well or poorly in those subjects.

What subjects did you like best? like least? If the job involves a good deal of math and you did poorly in math and did not like math, you shouldn't consider taking the job. If you enjoyed schoolwork related to what the job calls for, make sure to tell the interviewer about your interest in those courses.

Tell me about your extracurricular activities. Most students participate in some clubs or teams. Tell what part you played in your group. If you were elected to an office, assigned a project, gave public talks, had roles in plays or concerts, won athletic awards, or in any other way did something over and above what other students did, let the interviewer know. In competition with other high school graduates for the same job, anything you can bring out that shows you are better will help you get the job.

What part-time or summer jobs did you hold? If you worked while in high school, describe the jobs you held, tell how many hours you worked each week, and any promotions or special factors about the job that make you look good. For example, "I worked in a supermarket twenty hours each week. I started as a cashier on the checkout counter, but after only three months the manager promoted me to assistant bookkeeper. He said I earned the promotion because I was accurate, courteous to customers, and dependable."

Learn as much as you can about the job for which you are applying before going on the interview. If you can, ask people in the firm or ask the employment agency or whoever referred you to this company to tell you what they know about it. If you cannot obtain any information about the job itself, try to learn about the type of job. For instance, it may involve working in an office doing clerical work in the accounting department. Before going on this interview, try to talk to somebody who works in any accounting office to get some idea of what is done in that type of job. This will enable you to answer questions more intelligently about how your interests and education will fit into the open position.

High school graduates should have the following information available when applying for any job:

Social security card
Working papers (if under 18)
Proof of age (if over 18)—a driver's license is considered OK
Proof of high school graduation (diploma or transcript)
Work history (if you have worked part time or summers)
    Name and address of employer
    Person for whom you worked
    Kind of business
    What you did (brief job description)
    Salary
    Reason for leaving
School background
    Name and address of each school attended

Subjects taken
Grades
Extracurricular activities

COLLEGE GRADUATES

Many of the questions asked a high school graduate will also be asked of a college graduate. If you skipped the preceding section because you are a college graduate, go back and read it. You will probably be asked to describe your high school background as well as your college experience. Questions on grades, part-time work, and extracurricular activities in both high school and college should be expected.

What did you learn in college that would prepare you for the job for which you are applying? If you majored in the subject that is most pertinent to the job, describe the courses you took and indicate their relationship to the desired job. For example, the job is in the marketing department of a company. You majored in marketing. A good discussion could follow about the specific courses taken, projects on which you worked, or papers you wrote related to marketing.

But if you did not major in a related subject, analyze the job and determine what you did learn that would be applicable. For example, a marketing job requires communications skills and analytical skills. You can discuss how work you did in college demonstrated your proficiency in those skills.

Discuss some of your term papers, theses or special projects. Be prepared to talk about these in relationship to the type of position desired. Give specific examples of some of these and bring a few samples of pertinent papers to illustrate your work.

What courses did you start and later drop? Why? If your record is one of dropping hard courses and substituting easy ones, it will work against you. Give good reasons for dropping courses, such as, "It was not what I expected, so I took another course more in line with my interests."

Why did you choose to major in . . .? If the major is related to the job, express your long-term interest in this work. If it was not related to the job, talk about your interest in your major and how you felt it would help in any vocational area in which you might later become interested. For example, "I majored in history because I had not as yet decided on a career area and the research tools I would learn, plus the discipline of writing concise reports, would be helpful in any profession or management position."

Expect situational questions as discussed in Chapter 5. Persons with little work experience are often asked how they would handle hypothetical problems that may arise on a job.

What can you contribute to this job if you were to be hired? Don't give the impression you have all the answers even if you studied in college similar situations to what the job requires. Always indicate your willingness to learn, and point out that with your analytical skills or ability to learn rapidly, plus your technical training in computers or chemistry or economics or whatever, you believe you can become productive rapidly. Any leadership role you played in college or in part-time or other jobs should be brought out.

Here are some examples of poor and good responses to typical questions:

INTERVIEWER: Tell me about your experience in your summer job as a store adjustment clerk.

APPLICANT: *Poor:* I took care of customers' complaints about returned merchandise.
Better: I handled customer returns on a broad range of merchandise and did a good job of keeping the customers happy.

INTERVIEWER: What did you like best about your last job?

APPLICANT: *Poor:* There was not much supervision. I worked at my own pace.
Better: I was allowed to work on my own and could make decisions based on my own judgment.

Before answering any question, think carefully. If you properly prepare for an interview by reviewing your background thoroughly and analyzing how it fits into the job for which you are applying, it is much easier to answer questions than if you go unprepared to an interview. As stated previously, rehearsing the interview with persons who have some background in the field for which you are applying will be very helpful.

Proper preparation will prevent making some off-the-cuff comment which might negate all the good things previously brought out. Once a statement is made, it cannot be expunged from the record. Keep to the subjects asked; do not volunteer information unless you know it is an important asset you want the interviewer to be aware of and is related to the job. Casually mentioning that you led a demonstration against the administration of the university may show leadership ability, but more likely it will work against you.

WOMEN ENTERING OR RE-ENTERING THE WORK FORCE

Over the past several years, many women who have not worked in the business world for many years or have never worked at all have entered the job market. They often have skills and capabilities that are valuable to employers but do not have specific experience to qualify them for the positions for which they apply. However, many of these women have obtained excellent experience through part-time work, volunteer assignments, and education. If you are one of these women, examine your background carefully, using the Personal Background Organizer (see chapter 2). Some questions you might expect include the following:

When you were in school what courses did you take that qualify you for the position you seek? What have you done since leaving school to keep up with these skills? If you took secretarial studies in school ten years ago, but have either taken a recent refresher course or have practiced your steno and typing regularly, bring this point out. Perhaps you majored in economics in college and have recently taken a night course in finance—make sure the interviewer is told this fact. Other proofs of keeping up with the state of the art in your field would include reading professional journals and attending association meetings, seminars, or programs. Be prepared to discuss these with the interviewer.

If you have had previous work experience—even if it was some years ago—you may be asked to describe those jobs. Give details of your duties and responsibilities, what you liked and disliked about them, and most of all what you learned in your early career that would be helpful to you in the position for which you are applying.

What part-time jobs have you held in recent years? If these jobs were related to the desired position, tell how they helped you prepare to move into the full-time job you really want. If they were unrelated, indicate how they brought you into contact with business after being away and what you learned in each job that might be helpful. For example, "In my early job in marketing research, I did considerable work in survey evaluations. But that was before computers were used to the extent they are now. In my part-time job with the XYZ company, I had the chance to learn how computers and word processors were used. Now I am ready to return to my career in market research, with the added knowledge I acquired."

Tell me about your activities in volunteer work. This can be a major asset in your job search. Much work done by volunteers can be translated into job-related activities. Discuss your activities in fund raising, organizing, administration, and public contact. Tell what offices you held; what functions your job required you to coordinate, direct, and control; how you motivated others to do their jobs; and any other functions or responsibilities that illustrate your capabilities. For instance, "As chairperson of the Community Chest last year, I set up a program to reach every home in the community by phone and letter. I wrote the letter, organized a group of women to type addresses on the envelopes, worked with the printer to get the letters printed, and we had them all in the mail on the date scheduled. This was followed up by a telephone team, which I helped train. It resulted in collecting X thousand dollars, 13 percent more than the previous drive."

In your interview, keep the conversation on aspects of your background related to your accomplishments. Don't talk about your children, your husband, or family problems. If asked about family, keep the response to a minimum: "My children are all in school and I am free to pursue a job without concern about them" is all you should state. In chapter 9 we will discuss questions that are illegal to ask women and how you should handle them.

More and more women have made the transition from

full-time homemaker to full-time career person. Whether you are seeking an office or factory job or a professional or managerial position, you will have to be
prepared to point out why you are capable of performing the job sought. A careful self-evaluation will give you
the ammunition for such interviews. Pick from all the
things you have done in your life the accomplishments
which show your full potential and bring this out at your
interview. Here are some examples:

"My typing speed is fifty words per minute. I have
kept it up over the years since I last worked full time."

"Last year I raised X thousand dollars for my church.
This proves to me that I can get out there and sell."

"As a teacher's helper I was able to take over the
record keeping so the teacher could spend her time
teaching. This has given me experience in keeping
detailed records and I am confident I can keep similar
records in your firm."

CHAPTER 8

HANDLING OBJECTIONS TO YOUR BACKGROUND

Most applicants are not ideal candidates for the job for which they apply. There are some discrepancies between what the company wants and what the applicant offers. In addition, there may be negative aspects in our backgrounds that might have to be accounted for at an interview.

It is always advisable to have a good concept of what the job requirements are before going on an interview. If you have been referred to the company by an employment agency or by a friend who knows the company well, this information can be obtained from the referrer. If you have had a preliminary interview with the company, you can obtain this information from the interviewer before going on to the subsequent interviews for the job. If you do not have this advantage, you will have to determine what will probably be required from an analysis of the ad and from a general idea of what such positions usually require.

Study the specifications carefully and review your

background in light of these specifications. If you do not have some of the requirements, it does not mean you are not qualified. Often job specs are based on the "ideal" candidate and the company is willing to consider others who are not quite ideal. Determine what assets you have that would compensate for the missing requirements. By pointing out your strengths, you can show how they fit into the company's needs and therefore qualify you for the job. Let us examine several of these situations.

The position calls for a degree in business administration. You have a degree in liberal arts:

"I have had several courses that relate to business including two courses in economics and one in finance. I have also studied statistics and wrote a paper on marketing analysis for that course. My professors always complimented me on the conciseness and clarity of my reports, which I believe should be an asset to any business.

Or, "I do have a liberal arts degree, but I have been working in a position similar to the one you have open for three years. The experience in practical business applications acquired on this job—added to the research, analytical, and communication skills I developed in college—should help me do a superior job here."

The position calls for a college degree, but you did not graduate from college:

"Although I did not graduate from college, I took a number of courses and seminars in . . . and I do have very good work experience in this field."

Or, "I recognize the importance of college, but I was unable to afford to attend college when I graduated from high school. However, I have learned a great deal on the job and keep up with the state of the art in my field by reading the trade papers and attending seminars in this work regularly."

The job calls for five years experience and you have only three:

"As you know, the number of years' experience may not have a direct relationship to knowledge of the job. We all know people who have worked on a job for ten years and have only one year's experience. I was required to learn much about the job as fast as possible. I had a demanding boss and I acquired the skills he insisted upon very rapidly. I am sure I could meet your needs with the intensive experience I offer."

The job calls for very heavy experience in aspect A of the job, heavy experience in aspect B, and some experience in aspect C." *You are light in* A *and heavy in* B *and* C:

"It is true that I do not have as much of A as you would like; however, my strengths in B and C will enable me to perform those duties with little training, and my basic background in A will enable me to learn rapidly what I do not know already. When I started my current job, I knew nothing at all about B and C and was able to learn it and become productive in a very short time."

In addition to objections raised about specific deficiencies in your background related to job specs, there may be objections about other parts of your background.

You were fired for inability to perform your last job:
"I did not have the technical know-how for that position. I bit off more than I could chew. However, after discussing this position with you, I am sure it is within the scope of my skill and experience."

You were fired because of a "personality conflict" with your boss:
"I tried my best to work with Mrs. Grant, but she was never satisfied. I lasted six months in her department, which was longer than any of my predecessors."

You have not worked for over a year:

"When I was layed off the market for persons with my skills was very poor. I have been diligently trying to find a job, but have had no luck. I am anxious to work and I believe I can do a good job for your company if you give me the chance."

Or, "I decided to take a year off to travel. I couldn't afford to do this when I graduated from college and I believed it would be an important part of my education to see some of the world before settling down. I had a fantastic year seeing Europe and the Near East. I believe it gave me a comprehensive view of the world situation. I am now anxious to renew my career and am committed to working hard to meet my career goals."

Your school grades were poor:

"My grades and my interests have always gone hand in hand. I find that if I am interested in a subject I do well in it. If you will look over my transcript you will note that I achieved good grades in some tough subjects such as math and physics. I was interested in them and I worked hard. I have a similar interest in this job and I am sure I can do well in it, too."

Your previous experience has been in an entirely different type of work:

"For the past five years I have given all of my efforts and energies to the field of _____. I realize now that I am not interested in spending the rest of my life in that career. I gave it a fair shake, but it was wrong for me. However, I acquired a good deal of transferable skills in that work which can be applied to the job for which I am applying. They include. . . ."

You have an unstable work record:

"I understand your concern over my work record. I have had four jobs over the past five years. It does not look good. However, the reasons for leaving each job were beyond my control. The Aerospace Materials Company failed to get a large contract they had hoped for so those of us who were to work on that project were let go, and the Simpson Company was a new firm. Had they succeeded I would have been in on the ground floor, but they were undercapitalized and went out of business."

Or, "You will note that each of these jobs was in a different type of work. I have been exploring various careers and recognized shortly after taking the first three of these jobs that they were wrong for me, so I left after a few months. My most recent job was exactly what I wanted. Unfortunately, after one year the company went out of business. Your job is in this field and I know it is one in which I can be happy and successful."

The salary of the job for which you are applying is less than what you have been earning:

"Inasmuch as your salary is less than I have been earning, you may be wondering if I am seriously interested in this as a permanent job or am only looking for a standby position until I can get a higher-paying job. This is a natural concern. However, in my last job I earned much more than the usual salary for that kind of work because I was an innovator and producer. I started at a low salary and earned every increase by my personal productivity. The company wanted me to move out of town with them, but family reasons require me to remain here. I do not expect as high a salary to start but I know I can produce and earn the right for increases by my contribution to your company."

Some objections in the minds of the interviewer are never expressed. Indeed, some of those mentioned above are often the main reason for a rejection, and yet the interviewer does not bring them out in the interview. If you know you have some negatives in your background, do not assume that just because the interviewer has not asked about them, he or she has ignored them. Hidden objections are more dangerous than overt ones. You can always counter an objection if it is verbalized, but how can you overcome those that are not brought out into the open? It is your responsibility to point out those concerns that may stand in your way of getting the job and counter them at the same time. For example, if your less-than-average grades are not mentioned and you know the interviewer has reviewed your transcript, comment that you are not proud of your grades, explaining that in your early years you were not a serious student. Then talk about your improvement in grades, your higher grades in subjects of interest, etc.

Appearance, as we have said, makes a significant impression on an interviewer. Suppose you have an appearance problem that may hinder you from getting the job you want. For example, you are very short and in the past you have been rejected for sales jobs because the employer believes tall people are more impressive. Don't ignore your shortness. Bring it out in the interview. Tell how being short has helped you become more assertive and indicate in what other ways this has been a help instead of a hindrance.

If you have a speech defect, it is obvious that it will not be ignored by the interviewer. Bring out the fact that although the stammer is distracting, it is exacerbated by the nervousness caused by an interview and tends to disappear after you settle into a job. Also, if the job does not call for much talking, point out that your speech defect has never interfered with success on previous jobs or in school.

You are a woman and applying for a job that has traditionally been a "man's job." Because of sex discrimination laws, it is unlikely that this will be brought out by the interviewer, yet he may have hidden objections to a woman for this position. You might then say, "I am aware that usually men do this work, but I have had considerable training and experience in this field, and in all of my past associations I have worked well with both men and women. My boss in my last position will be happy to verify that he had reservations about a woman doing this kind of work, but after I was assigned to the job, he changed his mind."

Some hidden objections are not easily uncovered. They may not have any logic and may not fit into a specific problem in your background. They are in the mind of the interviewer. One way to uncover these objections is by carefully watching the responses—both verbal and nonverbal—of the interviewer. If the interviewer hesitates or raises his or her eyebrows after you have made some claim or statement, it might well indicate that he or she does not believe you. Do not ignore this. Either reiterate your statement with additional proof, or ask if he or she has any questions about it. For example, you indicate that you saved your company $30,000 by a system you developed. The interviewer appears skeptical. Immediately, repeat, "I saved the company the $30,000 by . . . (and then specify just how you did it)."

If, when reviewing your application form, the interviewer makes a casual comment on something you have written which you feel may indicate a reservation on his or her part, even though it is not overtly stated, ask if he or she has any questions about that point that you could clarify.

A daring approach that could be used if you feel that there is something that is bothering the interviewer about you which you cannot identify is to ask directly, "Is there anything about my background that gives you some concern about my qualifications for performing this job? If so, I would like to be able to discuss it with you, rather than let it fester unresolved in your mind."

It is far better to get things out in the open than to be rejected for a reason that may not have any validity. The assertive applicant must look for such problems and have them resolved before the interview is concluded.

CHAPTER 9

DEALING WITH ILLEGAL QUESTIONS (FOR WOMEN, MINORITIES, AND THE HANDICAPPED)

Federal and state laws on equal employment opportunity prohibit employers from asking certain questions of applicants which might cause discrimination in employment. Most employers are carefully trained to avoid asking such questions on an application form or in the interview, but occasionally interviewers may not be aware that the questions they are asking are illegal. In some cases, interviewers may deliberately ask such questions despite the laws. What do you do if you feel the question is illegal and will mitigate against your obtaining the job.

Before this problem can be discussed, it is important for you to know just what specific types of questions are legal and which types of questions are not. It would be embarrassing and probably fatal to your chances of getting a job if you claimed a legal question was illegal and refused to answer it.

On pages 150–154 is a chart prepared by the New York State Division of Human Rights indicating which questions are accepted and which are not in New York State. This chart is a good guide to *all* state and federal laws, although there may be some variation of a minor nature in other states. Attorneys and experts in this field use the New York guidelines as a standard applicable most everywhere, so you will be fairly safe to consider them as a viable model.

The questions in the chart are applicable only to preemployment inquiries. Once you are hired by a company, it may ask you many of the "unlawful" questions because this information may be needed for job-related purposes such as providing insurance, health benefits, pension plans, etc. The federal government is allowed to ask some questions that private business and state and local governments cannot. If applying for a federal job, some of the "illegal" questions in the chart may be allowed (e.g., citizenship, age, birthplace).

How does one handle an unlawful question that appears on the application form? If the application asks for information which you believe is unlawful, do not answer it. However, do not just leave it blank, but put a dash or the letters *N/A* (not applicable) in the space. If the interviewer should ask you why you did not answer it, state "As this question is no longer lawful and has no bearing on my qualifications for this job, I did not answer it." Remember, whenever responding to a question of this sort, keep your voice even and calm. Show no indication of indignation, protest or upset. Treat it, as it should be, as an accepted fact. If an employer insists that

LEGAL AND ILLEGAL PRE-EMPLOYMENT QUESTIONS

Here is a series of questions which the New York State Division of Human Rights has compiled as being lawful and unlawful pre-employment inquiries. As New York appears to be stricter than most states and the federal government, by following these recommendations, lawyers suggest that a company may be less likely to find itself in difficulty with the authorities because of pre-employment inquiries.

SUBJECT	LAWFUL*	UNLAWFUL
Race or Color		Complexion or color of skin. Coloring.
Religion or Creed:		Inquiry into applicant's religious denomination, religious affiliations, church, parish, pastor or religious holidays observed.
		Applicant may not be told "This is a (Catholic, Protestant, or Jewish) organization."
National Origin:		Inquiry into applicant's lineage, ancestry, national origin, descent, parentage or nationality.
		Nationality of applicant's parents or spouse.
		What is your mother tongue?

Sex:		Inquiry as to sex.
		Do you wish to be addressed as Mr.? Mrs.? Miss? or Ms.?
Marital Status:		Are you married? Are you single? Divorced? Separated?
		Name or other information about spouse.
		Where does your spouse work?
		What are the ages of your children, if any?
Birth Control:		Inquiry as to capacity to reproduce, advocacy of any form of birth control or family planning.
Age:	Are you between 18 and 70 years of age? If not, state your age.	How old are you? What is your date of birth?
Disability:	Do you have any impairments, physical, mental, or medical, which would interfere with your ability to perform the job for which you have applied?	Do you have a disability?
	If there are any positions or types of positions for which you should not be considered, or job duties you cannot perform because of physical, mental or medical disability, please describe.	Have you ever been treated for any of the following diseases . . .?

SUBJECT	LAWFUL*	UNLAWFUL
Arrest Record:	Have you ever been convicted of a crime? (Give details)	Have you ever been arrested?
Name:	Have you ever worked for this company under a different name?	Original name of an applicant whose name has been changed by court order or otherwise.
	Is any additional information relative to change of name, use of an assumed name or nickname necessary to enable a check on your work record? If yes, explain.	Maiden name of a married woman.
		If you have ever worked under another name, state name and dates.
Address or Duration of Residence:	Applicant's place of residence.	
	How long a resident of this state or city?	
Birthplace:		Birthplace of applicant.
		Birthplace of applicant's parents, spouse or other close relatives.
Birthdate:		Requirement that applicant submit birth certificate, naturalization or baptismal record. Requirement that applicant produce proof of age in the form of a birth certificate or baptismal record.

152

Photograph:		Requirement or option that applicant affix a photograph to employment form at any time before hiring.
Citizenship:	Are you a citizen of the United States?	Of what country are you a citizen?
	If not a citizen of the United States, do you intend to become a citizen of the United States? If you are not a United State citizen, have you the legal right to remain permanently in the United States? Do you intend to remain permanently in the United States?	Whether an applicant is naturalized or a native-born citizen; the date when the applicant acquired citizenship.
		Requirement that applicant produce naturalization papers or first papers.
	Requirement that applicant state whether he or she has ever been interned or arrested as an enemy alien.	Whether applicant's parents or spouse are naturalized or native-born citizens of the United States; the date when such parents or spouse acquired citizenship.
Language:	Inquiry into languages applicant speaks and writes fluently.	What is your native language?
		Inquiry into how applicant acquired ability to read, write or speak a foreign language.
Education:	Inquiry into applicant's academic, vocational or professional education and the public and private schools attended.	

SUBJECT	LAWFUL*	UNLAWFUL
Experience:	Inquiry into work experience.	
Relatives:	Name of applicant's relatives, other than a spouse, already employed by this company.	Names, addresses, ages, number or other information concerning applicant's spouse, children or other relatives not employed by the company.
Notice in Case of Emergency:		Name and address of person to be notified in case of accident or emergency.
Military Experience:	Inquiry into applicant's military experience in the Armed Forces of the United States or in a State Militia. Inquiry into applicant's service in particular branch of United States Army, Navy, etc.	Inquiry into applicant's general military experience.
Organizations:	Inquiry into applicant's membership in organizations which the applicant considers relevant to his or her ability to perform the job.	List all clubs, societies and lodges to which you belong.

*Inquiries which would otherwise be deemed lawful may, in certain circumstances, be deemed as evidence of unlawful discrimination when the inquiry seeks to elicit information about a selection criterion which is not job-related and which has a disproportionately burdensome effect upon the members of a minority group and cannot be justified by business necessity.

154

you respond to the omitted question, use your own judgment as to whether to answer or not. However, if you do not desire to answer it, simply state, "I didn't answer the question about my age because this information is no longer lawful and has no bearing on my qualifications for this job." The interview might then continue as follows:

INTERVIEWER: We must have this information on all applications.

APPLICANT: I am sure you do not wish to violate the age discrimination law. If you should hire me, I will be happy to provide proof of age for your benefits programs.

If the unlawful question is asked at the interview, you must be prepared to respond without anger or emotion. The following discussion explains several of the typical illegal questions asked and ways to handle them.

SEX DISCRIMINATION

What does your husband do? This question is illegal because often women have been rejected from jobs because it appears from their husband's job that he might be subject to transfer. For example, he is in the military service or works for a company that has a reputation for frequent transfers of personnel. You might reply, "My husband is in the computer field." You need not go further, and it is not necessary to identify his employer. Or, "My husband and I each have our own careers. I am sure that talking about *my* career will be more interesting to you."

What provisions have you made to take care of your children when you are at work? Simply answer, "My children are in good hands. I wouldn't think of pursuing a career without making adequate arrangements." It is not necessary to go any further.

How does your husband feel about your having a career? A good response is, "I have been working for several years, and this issue has not arisen." You may be tempted to tell the interviewer that this is none of his or her business, but if you want the job you have to keep your cool. Becoming upset about these questions will only "prove" to the interviewer that women are emotional and should not be given responsible assignments.

Are you separated or divorced? Are you a single parent? Neither of these questions is lawful. You may point this out and state, "You will note that my record of success in my previous jobs shows that I have been able to handle my work more than efficiently. Any personal problems I might have had have always been subordinate to my work."

I notice that you are wearing an engagement ring. When do you plan to be married? The employer is probably concerned about your needing time off for an imminent wedding. If you do require time off soon after your employment, it is only ethical to indicate this. However, if the wedding date is far off and although this is an illegal question (men do not wear engagement rings and therefore it is unlikely that this question would be asked of them), state, "We are not planning to be married until late next year." And add with a smile, "By that time I'll have earned some vacation time."

What are your plans for raising a family? Questions about family planning, use of birth-control methods, and similar inquiries are, of course, illegal. Such questions must be ignored or explicitly rejected: "I think it would be much more valuable to discuss how I can contribute to the success of this company."

Women often face hidden objections. The employer does not believe a woman could perform the type of job for which the applicant is applying. It has always been a "man's job." As pointed out in the previous chapter, even if it is not verbalized, if you feel this objection is standing between you and the job, bring it out yourself: "When I first started in this type of work, I was the only woman in my company—indeed, in the area—repairing typewriters. I not only became an expert in this work, but customers specifically requested that I be assigned to their accounts." Or, "You seem concerned about my ability to supervise men. I have had an enviable record of success in managing both men and women."

OTHER AREAS OF DISCRIMINATION

There are very few illegal questions specific to race discrimination. Most of the areas of concern are not verbalized. A black candidate for a position, for example, may feel that the company may consider his or her race a detriment in performing the job. This is particularly true when the job calls for meeting the public or supervising persons of other races. To overcome this, it may be advisable to bring out that you have previously been successful in the specific area in which the employer has some concern: "In my last job I supervised white, black, and hispanic people." "I thought I might meet resistance from white customers, but it was not too long before they accepted me with no qualms. My record of sales testifies to this."

Religious discrimination often revolves about the requirement in the law that companies provide accommodation for the religious practices of employees. This usually means giving them time off to observe religious holidays or their sabbath. Companies may not ask until after employment if such time off is needed. If asked directly if special time off is needed, most people who observe special sabbath days or holidays will say so, but it is not necessary at this point.

If you are required by your religion to wear a certain type of clothing (e.g., Mennonites or Hassidic Jews), the company cannot refuse to allow you wear it (unless there is a safety problem in certain types of facilities). Few interviewers will comment about this, but it may influence their decisions. A comment about your costume and how what you do or have done is more important than your outfit may alleviate the interviewer's concern.

The main concern facing applicants of foreign background is language. If you have an accent, it is possible that the interviewer may fear you do not understand or speak English well enough for the job. If your command of the language is adequate for the job, it will come out in the interview itself.

The equal employment laws have been interpreted to prohibit companies from asking about arrests. After all, a person is considered innocent until proven guilty, so why should an arrest which resulted in acquittal or dismissed charges be held against you? If asked about arrests, answer (if true), "I have never been convicted of a crime," and do not elaborate. If you do have a record of conviction, you are obligated to disclose it in most states. Some states prohibit asking about convictions that are in the distant past (e.g., New York State prohibits asking about any crime that was committed more than seven years earlier.). If you have a conviction, the company may still not refuse to hire you because of it unless it can show that the conviction is job related. For example, if you have been convicted of driving under the influence of alcohol, this should not ban you from a job that does not require driving. If you do have a conviction which you believe is not job related, answer, "Unfortunately, I have been convicted of driving under the influence of alcohol, but inasmuch as this job does not call for driving, it is not really pertinent. In any case, I have since stopped even social drinking."

THE HANDICAPPED

A relatively recent addition to the areas covered by equal opportunity laws is discrimination against the handicapped. If you are disabled, you are protected by the Rehabilitation Act of 1973 and various state laws. The handicapped should be prepared to answer questions related to their handicap, so long as such questions have real meaning regarding their ability to perform the job for which they are applying. A company is obligated to provide accommodations to assist the handicapped so that they can perform work that they might have previously been denied because of their disability. For example, companies must provide ramps so that persons using wheelchairs can get around a building. Deaf people should be given amplifying equipment so they can hear the telephone or take dictation from a dictating machine, etc.

If you are handicapped expect to answer such questions as the following:

For how long can you stand without assistance?
Can you read a sign on the wall?
Do you need any special equipment in order to perform the job?
Will it be necessary to have available any special medical equipment or medication (e.g., oxygen, insulin)?
Will you need to have any special help getting into or out of the building in case of fire or emergency?

These and related questions are lawful and necessary. However, a company may not refuse to hire you because you need special assistance.

The rehabilitation law also covers hidden disabilities —such as diabetes, epilepsy, chronic diseases—which will not be obvious to the interviewer. You are not required to divulge these to the employer unless you believe they are job related. Questions such as, "Do you have any disabilities?" or "Have you had any of a list of diseases?" are illegal. The company can only ask, "Do you have any disability or handicap that will prevent you from performing the job for which you are applying?" If asked this question, be frank and briefly explain your limitations.

Remember most employers are anxious to comply with the affirmative action provisions of the law and are making special efforts to recruit disabled persons. You have a much better than average chance of getting the job if you show confidence in your ability to handle it. Play up your abilities rather than your disabilities. Be prepared to show how you overcame your handicaps to accomplish things in previous jobs, school, or other activities. If the interviewer asks questions which you do not believe to be appropriate, diplomatically decline to answer them.

> **INTERVIEWER:** Has your being deaf hindered your social life?.
>
> **APPLICANT:** (with a smile) Social life and job life are not the same. I have never had problems dealing with fellow workers or supervisors in any job.

Blind persons using guide dogs should be sure to explain to employers that these dogs are so well trained they can stay with one individual all day on the job with no inconvenience to the company, customers, or other employees.

Minorities, women, and the handicapped must always keep in mind that it never pays to lose your temper or become belligerent if a question is asked which offends you. Most of the time it is due to the ignorance of the interviewer rather than any personal prejudice. It is never wise to threaten legal action. However, if the interviewer presses you to answer unlawful questions, a reminder that such questions are illegal and that you are not required to answer them is enough to stop the inquiries. Will such a response automatically cause the interviewer to reject you? We are dealing with human beings and it certainly may negatively affect some people, but because of the concern many companies have about litigation, many times it will work in your favor—at least to get you an interview with another person who may be more objective.

If you feel you have been discriminated against because of your race, religion, national origin, age, sex, or handicap, you can file complaints with your state human rights department (they vary in name from state to state) or with the local office of the Equal Employment Opportunity Commission. However, be sure you have a good case. Indicate the unlawful questions that were asked and any other evidence you have. Be sure you are really qualified to do the job or your claim will not be sustained. Most of the time, it is not necessary to make a legal complaint. By selling yourself positively, you will usually be able to overcome any reservations the employer may have.

CHAPTER 10

QUESTIONS YOU SHOULD AND SHOULD NOT ASK THE INTERVIEWER

At some time before the end of the interview, most employers tell the applicant something about the company and the job. Usually they give the applicant a chance to ask them some questions. This is your chance to clarify some of the factors related to the job that may not be clear to you, enabling you to obtain meaningful information to help you make the decision as to whether this is the right job for you.

Caution! The employer is using this section of the interview not only to give you information but also as another technique to measure you on the basis of the types of questions asked. To make a favorable impression, ask only those questions related to the job itself, and not those of a personal nature.

QUESTIONS YOU SHOULD ASK

If the duties and responsibilities of the job are not completely clear in your mind, here is your chance to ask specific details as to what your duties would be if you get the job. Questions of a specialized or technical nature for the particular job category are appropriate. For example:

Marketing: Would this job involve dealing directly with customers or just with the data provided by them?

Engineering: On what projects would I be working immediately? Over the next few years?

Accounting: Is your inventory based on LIFO or FIFO?

Computers: You did not mention whether you purchase packaged software or develop your own.

Personnel: How long does your contract with the union run before the next negotiation?

Office: What type of word-processing equipment are you contemplating purchasing?

Questions of a specific nature not only are helpful to you but also show the employer that you have enough knowledge of the field to ask the right questions.

If it has not been already discussed, ask to whom you would report and where you and your boss fit into the organization. Encourage the interviewer to show you an organizational chart and point out your position in relation to others in the department and the company.

Regarding training, you can ask, "What training will the company give me when I start?" Follow this through with questions on continuing training over the years and, if pertinent, what outside training such as additional schooling, seminars, and advanced degrees would help your growth in the organization. A person who is interested in self-improvement—particularly as related to his or her job—makes a very strong impression.

Most, but not all jobs lead directly to higher positions. It is good to ask about what these positions will be and how long one might expect to be in each job before promotion is warranted: "What is the normal progression from this job?"

Questions about the company are also appropriate. You may ask about the company's gross sales; market share; plans for growth, for acquisitions, and for introducing new products or services. If you have not already seen an annual report, you may ask for a copy. (If the company is a public company, annual reports are usually available; if it is privately held, do not ask for an annual report, as it is not usually published).

Other questions you might ask about the company:

Who are your chief competitors?
Who are some of your best customers?
How many employees are there in the company, this facility?

If the company has branches in other locations, it is important to ask if the company usually transfers people from one location to another. If relocation at a future time might be a problem for you, it is best to know about it before deciding to work for that company.

Other questions you might want to ask about the job for which you are being considered:

Is the job currently filled?
Why is it now open?
How long was it before each of the former holders of this job was promoted?
Do you transfer people from one job to another laterally in the company? Under what circumstances?
How much travel does this job entail?
What can I do to become immediately productive in this job?

Before going to the interview, prepare at least three or four questions about the specific nature of the job as related to your background. Frame these questions in such a way to show you have done your homework, are familiar with the basic needs of the company, and have the technical or specialized background required in this job. The more specific you are, the better it is. For example, if you are applying for a position in personnel and you learn before going to the interview that a union is attempting to organize the company, you may ask, "What steps have you taken in your campaign to defeat the union drive?" Or better, if applicable, you could say, "In my last company, I headed a campaign to defeat a union organization drive. I'm interested in what you have been doing." If you are an office manager and you understand that the company is in the process of computerizing its records, you might say, "Having recently gone through the computerization of records in my present job, I'm interested in what special problems you are having in this area?"

By tying in your background in a facet of the work that the company is currently facing, you add strength to your candidacy.

QUESTIONS YOU SHOULD NOT ASK

Because you are judged by the type of questions asked, it is important to avoid asking questions that might make you appear to be unbusinesslike or unprofessional in your approach to the company. Such questions, as "When can I expect my first raise?" or "I know it is already May, but will I get a vacation this summer?" reflect your selfish concerns. If it is necessary for you to have some time off within a few months after you are hired for a very important reason (like getting married), once the job is offered and accepted, bring it up. Most companies will agree, but do not let this be a factor while you are still being considered for the job and final decision has yet to be made.

Many applicants are concerned about benefits that may be offered by the company—and these are important. However, it is not smart to ask about them at this point in the interview. Most employers will tell you about benefits before they make a final offer. Some even provide written statements of the benefits program. Concern about medical, insurance, or pension plans is natural, but should be held back until the very end of the negotiations.

Benefits of a professional nature such as tuition reimbursement for courses taken to improve your skills, participation in professional or business associations might be interpreted positively. Interest in these benefits are interpreted as a desire to learn and improve your skills rather than a selfish concern.

Young people, particularly recent college graduates, may interrogate a prospective employer about their activities on social issues. Idealistic youngsters may want to know what the company is doing about pollution in the environment, ecology, race relations, investments in companies engaged in nuclear energy, or activities in South Africa or other countries. No matter what your own political beliefs are, the job interview is no place to expound on them or to debate the interviewer on his or her company's attitudes. It will almost always leave a negative feeling about you.

Do not ask questions of the interviewer about matters the company may consider confidential. Privately held companies often do not divulge sales figures and profit or loss information. You might preface questions on these matters with, "If it is not kept confidential by your company, I would be interested in. . . ."

Before going to an interview, learn as much as possible

about the company. From what you have learned from your research, you can frame a series of pertinent questions that not only will give you better knowledge of your prospective employer, but will also impress the interviewer with your knowledge of the organization and the intelligence of the questions you ask. Asking questions can be a key factor in the decision as to whether you will or will not get the job, so think carefully about what you ask, and be sure that your questions reflect your good judgment and capabilities.

CHAPTER 11

NAILING DOWN THE JOB

At the early interviews your objective is usually to make a strong enough impression to be invited for a subsequent interview. Your overall objective is, of course, to get a job offer, and this must always be in mind. Some jobs may be closed at the first interview, but most usually require two or three interviews with different people before the decision is reached.

The interviewer usually controls the timing of the interview and determines when it should end. You must keep alert to his or her verbal and nonverbal actions to know when the end is approaching. Some clues to this:

- You are asked if you have any more questions.
- You are asked how you feel about the situation.
- The interviewer pushes him/herself away from the desk.
- The interviewer closes the folder in which your resume and application are filed.
- The interviewer stands up.

If this is a preliminary interview, when you note a closing cue, accept it and do not try to extend the interview by continuing to talk. You may ask a final question and make a final brief statement, but a lengthy speech at this point could reverse a favorable decision and is unlikely to change an unfavorable one: Ask, "Is there anything else I can tell you about myself?" Comment, "I am very interested in this job and look forward to hearing from you further."

At subsequent interviews when you have a better picture of the job and how you stand in the competition for it, you can be more assertive. By this time you know just what has most interested the employer about your background and how you can contribute to the company's goals. In closing these interviews, play up the areas that you know are of particular interest:

"My experience in analyzing costs would fit well into your new program for cost reduction."

"Just as I did with the XYZ Company, I can develop business in the paper industry for your product."

"I look forward to the challenge of. . . ."

"I've faced tough problems like the ones you have mentioned over and over again in my career and have licked them."

As an interview is a two-way street, it is also important for you to understand just what is expected of you if you should be hired. Most employers welcome questions of a specific nature on duties and responsibilities, problems that will have to be faced, and other aspects of the work. In the preceding chapter, we gave examples of this. Before leaving an interview in which job duties have been discussed, ask any questions needed to clarify your understanding of the job. Intelligent and meaningful questions at this time will solidify your position and let the employer know you are knowledgeable about the job and interested in it.

NEGOTIATING SALARY

One of the most important parts of the interview is the negotiation of salary. In many jobs, particularly at the lower levels, there is no negotiation. The company has established a salary and it is a take-it-or-leave-it proposition. If you are in such a situation, it is important to have a good idea of what that salary is before going too far. Most firms will ask you your desired salary on the application form, and if it is not in line with their budget, they will bring it up early in the interview. It is best for you to try to learn about salary ranges before going for the first interview. This is not easy unless you have been referred by an employment agency or someone who knows the company well. However, if your salary is very much out of line with what the company intends to pay, it usually comes out early in the hiring procedure, and you will either be eliminated or the subject will be brought up.

Assuming you are in the company's range, the specific amount of salary will have to be determined before the offer is made and accepted. To understand how such decisions are made it is helpful to examine the factors considered by employers.

Most important is the salary range established for this job by the company. This range may or may not have any relationship to your current salary or desired income. It has been developed by evaluating the job in relation to other jobs in the company.

Equally important is the "going rate" for personnel in the job category. This rate is determined by the supply and demand of people with the skills required. For example, if secretaries are in short supply in a community, salaries for secretaries will be higher than in communities where there is no shortage. This will require companies in the community with a short supply to raise the salary range for secretaries if they want to attract personnel.

Within the range that a company will pay, the salary offered to any one individual will depend on that person's experience and other qualifications. Persons with several years' experience or advanced education can command higher salaries than those with less.

Another consideration is current salary. If you are earning a salary below the bottom of the range, you most likely will be offered a starting pay at the bottom of the range. If you are making more money, you can command a higher salary on the new job. This is not always equitable because the applicant may have been working in an industry or in a company where salaries are generally lower than the norm for other industries or communities. Often, women have been paid lower salaries than men for the same type of work. If the new salary is based on the old, this will perpetuate the differential in men's and women's salaries.

Another factor is the negotiating strength of the individual or, if there is a labor union involved, the negotiating efforts of that union. In the latter case there is not much any applicant can do to determine his or her salary. But if one can negotiate on one's own, this can be a key factor.

To prepare for your negotiation, you should know the range the company has for the job. This usually will be discussed once the company has indicated interest in you for the position. You should know the going rate for jobs in your category. You can obtain this from newspaper ads, discussions with others in the field, your own experience, and employment agencies in the community.

If you are within the range and are currently earning a salary that is equitable, feel free to ask for 10 to 15 percent above your current earnings. If there is a shortage of people in your type of work, you can freely ask for 20 to 30 percent above current salary. Anything above will probably be rejected unless you are so valuable to the company that you can write your own ticket.

If you are made an offer which you consider too low, do not turn down the job immediately. Either make a counteroffer at an acceptable salary or ask what else the job offers in terms of benefits, opportunity for salary increases in the future, and other compensation such as bonuses or a company car. Be sure you know the whole package before you reject an offer.

Ask why the offered salary was below what you expected. If the answer is that it is based on your current salary and you believe you are currently underpaid, you might say, "The main reason I am leaving my job is that I have been underpaid. The salary I request is in line with the market for my skills" Or, "If I remain where I am I will get an increase that will bring me up to the salary you offer. I would like to work for your company, but there is no financial benefit to me unless the salary is at least. . . ."

It is important to indicate that you really would like to accept the job but cannot do so at the money offered. Give the company a chance to review its offer and ask for a decision within a reasonable time. If the company cannot meet your salary requirements, but you feel it still is worthwhile to take the job because of other benefits— e.g., financial—tell the company that and ask when reviews of salary are made. If you will have to work at a lower salary than you need for any length of time, it may still not be advisable to accept the offer. Unless there are no opportunities for persons with your experience available, it is often better to reject a job which will put you in a financial hole. A bit more patience may turn up a better spot.

EMPLOYMENT CONTRACTS

Very few persons outside of the top executive ranks are given employment contracts. In some industries, contracts are more commonly used than others. Most people will be hired on a verbal offer and acceptance. Occasionally, you may receive a letter to confirm the verbal offer, but it is not usual for most jobs. Engineers and other technical personnel are more likely to obtain formal letters of offer than others; salespeople who come from competitors and who can guarantee bringing business with them may be given employment contracts.

Unless you fit into one of these categories, it is not wise to ask for a contract; it will only be refused. However, if you are asked to sign a contract by the company, it is important that you have it scanned by an attorney. The company may be restricting your freedom of action by this contract. Some companies ask persons who are dealing with customers to sign restrictive clause contracts which prohibit them from working for a competitor for a period of time after leaving that company. This may be a legitimate request or it may be unreasonable. It is important that you fully understand what it implies before signing it. This depends on how it is worded and what restrictions are made. Your attorney can interpret this for you in light of the laws in your state.

FOLLOW-UP

Often the job offer is not made when you expect it. You are told that you are a serious candidate, but the company is still interviewing. What can you do to expedite the decision and to keep yourself in the view of the interviewers?

At the end of the interview, be sure to express a serious

interest in the job. You may reinforce this by asking specifically for the job: "This is the kind of a job I know I can do superbly and contribute to your company's success. I would appreciate serious consideration for this job."

Salespersons and others whose assertiveness would be an asset in obtaining the job might be more aggressive: "When can I start? I'm ready and anxious to get started on this job."

A few days after each interview (unless the interviews closely follow one another), write a brief note to the person who interviewed you thanking him or her for the interview and reiterating your interest in the job. This note should remind the interviewer of who you are— especially if he or she is interviewing quite a number of applicants for the position. Emphasize a key aspect of your background that makes you stand out and exemplifies your qualifications for the job.

Letter after first interview:

Dear Miss Adams:
   Thank you for the courtesy extended to me at my interview for the position as marketing assistant last Thursday afternoon.
   My marketing project at New York University included a detailed study of the special problems in your industry and certainly familiarized me with the language, customs, and major competitors in the appliance field.
   This is a job I have confidence I can contribute to, and I look forward to an interview with your marketing director.

Letter after later interview:

Dear Mr. Turner:
   I appreciate the time you gave me out of your busy schedule Monday afternoon. The description of the work

your firm is doing was most helpful in enabling me to review my own qualifications in light of your needs.

There are several areas of similarity between what you need and what I have done. This is particularly true in the conversion of manual to computer systems. You will recall that this is one of the highlights of my background with my present employer.

I am preparing some material which will give you details of some of my work in this field. May I have the opportunity of seeing you again next week to show this to you?

Letter after final interview

Dear Ms. Cooper:

Thank you again for seeing me on Friday. The position we discussed is exactly where I can contribute most. I would appreciate your serious consideration of my candidacy for the office manager job. I am sure I will be a valuable addition to your management staff.

A few days after sending the letter, telephone the interviewer. Rather than ask, "How am I doing?" refer to the interview; remind the interviewer who you are by referring to one or more of your qualifications ("I am the man who worked for the ABC Co. as a draftsman") and ask, "Can I provide you with any additional information about my background?" Of course, if you have had several interviews or calls it is not necessary to identify yourself further. Always ask if the interviewer would like to see you again. If no additional information is needed, ask when you can expect to have a decision? Do not pester employers with frequent calls. A good procedure:

two days after interview: follow-up letter
two to three days later: telephone call to the interviewer
seven days later: a second call

If you do not hear after that, forget this job—unless you have been told to call again.

If you receive a rejection letter or a phone call, thank the company for its consideration and express interest in future openings if any should occur. Never shut the door completely. The person hired may not succeed and the job may open up again. Additional openings may develop in the near or not-too-distant future and you may be available. Again, a brief note to the interviewer is not out of line. Be brief and polite and express continuing interest.

> Dear Mr. Rockwell:
>
> Of course I was disappointed that I did not get the job as personnel assistant in your company. However, I appreciate the time you spent with me and the consideration you gave to my qualifications. If at some future time a similar position should open in your company, I would appreciate a chance to compete for it. Perhaps someday I can be a part of the XYZ company's team.

Ten Reasons Applicants are Rejected at an Interview (. . . and how to avoid them)

1. Poor interview manners.

Coming late to the interview almost always turns the interviewer off. If you are unavoidably delayed, phone the interviewer and let him or her know you will be late, or better still, ask for another appointment. Remember, the interviewer has other appointments and has other things to do.

Smoking when the interviewer is not a smoker is another turnoff. Keep your cigarettes in your pocket or purse unless the interviewer lights up and suggests that you may.

Be courteous. Follow the lead of the interviewer in when and where to sit, when to get up and leave.

2. Poor appearance.

Wear conservative clothes. Be sure your shoes are shined, your nails are clean, and your hair is combed. First impressions last, and appearance is the chief ingredient of the first impression. Neatness and cleanliness are automatic for most of us, but even a slight deviation can cause the applicant to lose the chance at a good job.

3. Unrealistic demands about the job.

Young people particularly are often unrealistic. They want to start at the top or take over running a department before they have earned the right to do so. When asked what you seek in the job, be realistic. Talk about opportunity to learn and eventually contribute, rather than giving the impression you can take over immediately and the current managers can retire.

4. Unrealistic salary demands.

Know what you are worth by studying the going rate for jobs in your skill area. Do not ask for more money than is being paid in the community unless there is a severe shortage of personnel with your skills. Asking for an unrealistic salary reflects poorly on your judgement.

5. Knowing little about the company.

Before the interview, research as much as you can about the company. Know at least what business they are in and, if possible, find out such things as sales volume, who its competitors are, product lines, share of market, and reputation in the industry. This information can be obtained from directories, talks with others in that industry, customers, and people who work or formerly worked for the company.

6. Talking too much at the interview.

Once you have made your point—shut up. Too many people talk so much they lose the attention of the listener. If your new job depends upon your ability to listen, you had better train yourself to listen and not talk.

7. Talking too little.

Don't let the preceding admonition prevent you from telling all you have to tell about your background. Answer each question fully. Be sure you give all the information requested. Before concluding your response, ask yourself if there is anything else of importance you should convey.

8. Being overly charming.

Some people get by on charm, but if overdone, it makes you look superficial. Tasteless humor, "clever" remarks, coyness, or coquettishness will tend to impress negatively rather than positively.

9. Being overly modest.

Don't be afraid to blow your own horn. Nobody else is there to do it for you. Tell about your accomplishments and what it meant to your employers. Tell about awards won, praise received, and contributions that paid off. This is your only chance to let the employer know you are better than your competitors for the job. Don't be held back by false modesty.

10. Lack of follow-up.

After the interview write a thank-you note to the person or persons who interviewed you. If you do not hear from the company in a week, phone them. But don't make a pest of yourself by frequent follow-up calls. Even if you are rejected, thank the company for consideration. It may lead to opportunities in the future.

GOOD LUCK IN YOUR JOB SEARCH.